The

AUGUSTINE *CATECHISM*

The Augustine Series

Selected writings from "The Works of Saint Augustine—
A Translation for the 21st Century."

Volume I

The Enchiridion on Faith, Hope, and Love

Saint Augustine

The
*A*UGUSTINE
*C*ATECHISM

The Enchiridion
on Faith, Hope, and Love

Translation and Notes by
Bruce Harbert

Introduction by
Boniface Ramsey, O.P.

Edited by
John E. Rotelle, O.S.A.

New City Press
www.newcitypress.com

Published in the United States by New City Press
202 Cardinal Rd., Hyde Park, NY 12538
www.newcitypress.com

Cover design by Nick Cianfarani
Cover illustration: Augustine at the Council of Carthage by Tito Troya,
Saint Augustine Church, Philadelphia, PA, USA

Library of Congress Cataloging-in-Publication Data:
  Augustine, Saint, Bishop of Hippo.
    [Enchiridion. English]
    The Augustine catechism : the enchiridion on faith, hope, and love
  / Saint Augustine.
      p. cm.
    Includes bibliographical references.
    ISBN 1-56548-124-0 (pbk.)
    1. Theology--Early works to 1800. I. Title.
  BR65.A73E5 1999
  230'.14--dc21   99-18777
                                                         CIP

We are indebted to Brepols Publishers, Turnholt, Belgium, for their use of the Latin
critical text for *Enchiridion ad Laurentium de Fide et Spes et Caritate,* ed. E. Evans, *Corpus
Christianorum Latinorum* 46 (Turnholt 1969) 49-114.

Nihil Obstat: John E. Rotelle, O.S.A., S.T.L., Censor Deputatus
Imprimatur: +Patrick Sheridan, DD, Vicar General, Archdiocese of New York
              Archdiocese of New York, December 11, 1998

1st printing: July 1999
4th printing: October 2003

Printed in Canada

Contents

The Enchiridion on Faith, Hope, and Love

Introduction

It is impossible to supply an exact date for the composition of the *Enchiridion* except to say that it was written sometime after the death of Jerome (which is alluded to in XXIII, 87) and before the composition of the treatise *The Eight Questions of Dulcitius* (which mentions the *Enchiridion* in 1, 10). Inasmuch as Jerome seems to have died in either 419 or 420, and inasmuch as the *Eight Questions* can very likely be dated to 422, it follows that our treatise was produced between 419 and 422.

At this point Augustine had already written, or was still in the process of writing, the works for which he is best known — the *Confessions*, *The Trinity*, and *The City of God*. The Manichean and Donatist controversies, to which he had devoted generous attention and which had given him the occasion to make enduring theological contributions, lay largely behind him. The struggle with Pelagianism, on the other hand, was in full swing and would continue unabated until his death in 430 at the age of nearly seventy-six. Whatever its exact date may be, then, the *Enchiridion* is in any event a work of Augustine's high maturity, produced when he was in his mid- to late sixties.

About the Laurence to whom the treatise is addressed we can venture relatively little. He is spoken of as the brother of Dulcitius in the book *The Eight Questions of Dulcitius* 1, 10, and *Revisions* II, 59 refers to Dulcitius himself as a tribune and notary who was in Africa "as the executor of the imperial orders handed down against the Donatists." This must mean, for want of anything more precise to say about him, that Laurence was a person of some consequence. The first words of the *Enchiridion* term Laurence learned and suggest that he is on the road to acquiring that wisdom which, according to Augustine, as we know from other contexts,[1] far surpasses mere learning or knowledge. This may, however, be nothing more than a bit of customary epistolary courtesy.

From both *Enchiridion* I, 6 and *Revisions* II, 63 it is clear that Laurence requested the work from Augustine. The latter has it: "He to whom the book was addressed had asked to have some little work of mine that would not leave his hands." That Augustine complied with Laurence's request calls to mind that this was an era (which perhaps only ended in modern times) when simpler folk could approach intellectual giants and ask such favors of them in the expectation that they would be granted. Many of Augustine's writings were produced in this way, at the behest of others. In fact, a letter that he wrote in response to a certain Dioscorus, who had importuned Augustine for information that Augustine himself considered vain and superfluous, expresses his willingness to answer all requests, despite his onerous responsibilities, so long as they are not improper.[2] This same letter gives the reader some glimpse of those responsibilities, which left the bishop of Hippo little time for the more studious pursuits that he really enjoyed, and it serves to underline how remarkable his readiness to comply with these requests was. In the end, after having complained (at length) to Dioscorus, Augustine fulfills his demands as well, foolish as they may have been, doubtless thinking that thereby he was accomplishing at least some good. The *Enchiridion*, on the other hand, betrays none of the reluctance that the letter to Dioscorus does. Here Augustine was performing a labor that he must have felt was in keeping with his intellectual mission. Indeed, even though Laurence wanted something rather short, Augustine eschewed too great a brevity as being inadequate to the seriousness of the matter that Laurence had asked him to address (I, 2-3). Of course, he knew that what he wrote to Laurence (but probably to Dioscorus also, for that matter) would not be restricted to the recipient's eyes but would be published and have a wider circulation.

Although Laurence may have wished for a more cursory treatment of his questions than that which Augustine eventually provided him, he was nonetheless not sparing in the number and scope of those that he posed. What is to be sought more than anything else? he wanted to know. What is to be avoided more than anything else? How are reason and faith related to each other? What is the beginning and the end of what should be held? How can Christian doctrine be summarized? What is a sure foundation of Catholic faith (I, 4.)? Augustine himself compresses all these questions into a single one when he says in I, 2: "Perhaps this is exactly what you wish me to explain briefly and to sum up in a few words: How is God to be worshiped?"

Augustine replies to his own question by asserting: "God is to be worshiped with faith, hope, and love" (I, 3). And he adds that once he has explained what the objects of these three virtues are — "what we should believe, what we should hope for, and what we should love" (*ibid.*) — he will have answered all Laurence's questions. (The pursuit of this theme is the reason for the more correct if less popular title of the work — *On Faith, Hope, and Love*. Augustine himself refers to it as such in *Revisions* II, 63: "I also wrote a book on faith, hope, and love. . . . " This "little work" [*opusculum*], he continues, is what the Greeks would call an *enchiridion*, a book that one could hold in one's hands,[3] which is what

Laurence wanted to have and which gave the treatise its familiar title.)

Of the three virtues upon which Augustine chose to focus in his response to Laurence, faith is far and away the one to which he devotes the most attention. The section on faith begins, it can be seen, at III, 9, and it concludes at XXIX, 113. The section on hope is XXX, 114-116, and that on love is XXXI, 117-XXXII.121. The disproportionate treatment is striking, particularly in view of the fact that love was a kind of "specialty" of Augustine's: it was a virtue that, along with humility, he bequeathed anew to the Christian tradition after it had first become part of that tradition through the authors of the New Testament. Augustine himself does not provide a clue as to why the three virtues were dealt with as they were, but two solutions suggest themselves. The first is that he did not feel that he could give a shorter account of faith — namely, the tenets of the Christian faith — than he actually did, and that, as a result, he had to compress his treatment of hope and love if he wanted to stay within the bounds of a handbook or *enchiridion*, of which he seems to have been quite conscious.[4] The second possible solution is that faith is discussed at greatest length because it is the most "teachable" of the three virtues, the most susceptible to being written about in a systematic way. Hope, on the other hand, is the most elusive of the three and could hardly but receive short shrift. And love could be appropriately handled with brevity if it were clear that, as the last of the three, it was also the greatest of them and their *raison d'être*. It is hard to say which of these solutions is the more likely, and of course perhaps neither is correct.

Before Augustine begins his discussion of the three virtues on a separate basis, one by one, he discusses them briefly together. Faith, he says, is the beginning of the

Christian life; it works through love and concludes with the vision of God, which represents the highest possible human happiness. This is the sum of Christian doctrine, and in defining it Augustine has answered one of Laurence's original questions. As for the foundation of faith (to address another of Laurence's questions), it is Christ, even though Christ's name may be claimed not only by the orthodox but even by heretics (I, 5).

The next few pages of the *Enchiridion* attempt to establish a relationship among the three virtues. They are similar in that all three pray — not only hope and love, as one might expect, but faith as well, because hope and love cannot exist without faith (II, 7). Neither, quite apart from the issue of prayer, can love exist without hope or hope without love. Faith alone can exist by itself, and in support of this position Augustine cites the unconsoling words of James 2:19: *Even the demons believe — and shudder* (II, 8).

With this to serve as a preliminary, Augustine now plunges into his treatment of faith. He had already mentioned the Creed in connection with the first of the three virtues in II, 7. Somewhat strangely, perhaps, however, he did not allude there to the fact that his discussion of faith would use the Creed as an outline. But the reader gradually becomes aware that the order of the Creed is being observed from III, 9 on, and then Augustine finally confirms this realization in XV, 56, and later in XVII, 64 and XXX, 114.

This was not the first time that Augustine had used the Creed as a basis for instruction in the faith. He had already done so in the *De fide et symbolo*, which was a sermon preached in the year 393; in the treatise *De agone christiano*, published about 396; and in Sermons 212-215, preached at different times. Moreover, other Fathers had done the same. The Creed was typically laid out in sermons delivered to those who were about to be baptized. This was the case with Augustine's Sermons 212-215 and also, to cite the most notable example, with the *Catecheses* of Cyril of Jerusalem. It made abundant sense to use this pedagogic vehicle, which lay so ready to hand.

At the time that Augustine was writing, several creeds would have been at his disposal. There was the great Nicene-Constantinopolitan Creed, the Apostles' Creed (on which Rufinus of Aquileia had published a commentary at the very beginning of the fifth century) and an indeterminate number of other creeds associated with particular episcopal sees. What creed might lie at the bottom of the *Enchiridion* it would be difficult to say with certitude, since Augustine, while following a credal order, alludes to a credal text rather than actually quoting one. Hippo, which was Augustine's own city, had its creed, and one would be tempted to think that the bishop of the place had used it. There is reason to believe, however, that he did not restrict himself to one creed but borrowed from two. The creeds of Hippo and Milan, where Augustine had lived for about four years and where he was baptized, may well have been his two sources; at least they represent two different kinds of creed from which Augustine could have drawn.

The Creed of Hippo, unlike that of Milan, refers to God the Father as creator, and Augustine devotes a significant amount of attention in the *Enchiridion* to the doctrine of creation (III, IV, 15). On the other hand, the Milanese Creed, as Augustine seems to know it (he cites it in Sermons 212-214), diverges from that of Hippo when it refers to the incarnation. The Creed of Hippo reads: "Credimus . . . in . . . Iesum Christum . . . natum de Spiritu sancto *ex* virgine Maria" (We believe . . . in . . . Jesus Christ . . . born of the Holy Spirit *from* the Virgin Mary"). But the Milanese Creed has: "Credo . . in Iesum Christum, . . qui natus est de Spiritu sancto *et* Maria virgine" ("I believe . . . in Jesus Christ, . .

who was born of the Holy Spirit *and* the Virgin Mary"). It is the latter, Milanese, version that Augustine reflects in X, 34 when he writes: " . . . ut crederemus in Dei . . . Filium natum de Spiritu sancto *et* Maria virgine" (" . . . that we may believe in the . . . son of God . . , born of the Holy Spirit *and* the Virgin Mary") (see also XII, 38). Another divergence between the two creeds occurs at the end of each. That of Hippo mentions the Church in its final words, whereas the Milanese mentions it immediately after the Holy Spirit. Here, again, Augustine seems to have employed the latter as his model inasmuch as he writes in XV, 56, after having said a few words on the Spirit: "Then we mention Holy Church. . . . Due order in the profession of faith required that the Church should be named after the Trinity. . . ."[5]

In any event, except for variations such as these, which could arguably be considered minor, many of the Latin creeds with which we are presently familiar would not have been inconsistent with Augustine's ordering of his material in the *Enchiridion*. As a sample of the typical creed we can conveniently cite one of the two that Augustine may have used, namely that of Milan, which reads as follows:

> I believe in God the Father almighty;
> and in Jesus Christ, his only Son, our Lord, who was born of the Holy Spirit
> and the Virgin Mary, suffered under Pontius Pilate, was crucified and was buried, ascended into heaven, sits at the right hand of the Father, whence he will come to judge the living and the dead;
> and in the Holy Spirit, the Holy Church, the forgiveness of sins, the resurrection of the flesh.[6]

The straightforwardness of this statement of faith, or whichever other one or ones that he might have used, did not evoke in Augustine a comparably straightforward response. Although he moved from point to point with the Creed, he did not do so with simplicity and directness. Rather, he addressed questions along the way that, although not unconnected with the matter at hand, would not have been missed had they not been raised. The modern reader might be inclined to take Augustine to task for what he or she might view as his digressiveness, but the author's contemporaries would have undoubtedly given very little thought to it: it was a style that they took for granted.

A good example in this regard is the discussion of error, lying, and skepticism that occupies nearly a tenth of the treatise, from V, 17 to VII, 22. It is to be found in the context of the treatment of the initial article of the Creed, on God the Father and on God's creative activity, and none of it could be characterized as directly related to that article. However, since faith is professed not in a vacuum but rather in a world marked by error, deceit, and doubt as to what can be reasonably assented to, all of which obviously have a bearing on the possibility of belief, it must have made sense for Augustine to raise the issue early on in his exposition of faith. Moreover, Augustine was particularly interested in the morality of lying, having written two books on the subject, the *De mendacio* and the *Contra mendacium*, the former in the 390's and the latter only shortly before the composition of the *Enchiridion*; and he revered the truth, as is evident in his references to Christ simply as "Truth."[7] This, then, was a theme that could well find its way into a work such as the *Enchiridion*, which had a certain comprehensive quality to it. But why so lengthy a section, from XIX, 70 to XX, 77, on almsgiving? Although it fits appropriately under the heading of the forgiveness of sins, the extent of its treatment seems unnecessary.

And what can explain the exclusion of other themes of at least equal importance, or the fact that some receive what might appear to us to be woefully inadequate treatment? For example, although baptism is the subject of considerable discussion, particularly in XIII, 42, XIV, 53, and in XIII, 46, XVII, 65 and XXII, 82-83 penance receives the attention that is commensurate with the infrequency of its practice in Christian antiquity (until about the sixth century there was only one opportunity after baptism itself for sacramental remission of sins), the eucharist is only alluded to twice, both times in passing and with extreme brevity (in XXIX, 110 and XXX, 115, the latter passage being outside the ambit of the section on faith). The lack of material on the eucharist is disappointing, but one may surmise that Augustine handles this sacrament as he does because it was not a theologically controverted topic. The meaning of baptism, on the other hand, had been called into question by the Pelagians, and hence it merited extensive treatment. The handling of the Church on earth (XV.56), in comparison to that of the Church in heaven (XV.57-XVI.63), also leaves something to be desired, particularly in light of Augustine's profound contributions to ecclesiology, and it is not easy to guess at his reasoning here.

We ought not, however, to be hard on Augustine for what he did not touch on so much, perhaps, as be grateful to him for what he did. Although the *Enchiridion* offered him a kind of comprehensive scope, we have no right to expect total inclusiveness. It may be that we have been misled in this regard by the popular title of the work: *Enchiridion* conjures up the names of Denzinger and Schönmetzer, the editors of the *ne plus ultra* of Church teaching, and nowadays a "handbook" can mean much, much more than it did in antiquity, as we may see from the multi-volume *Handbook of Church History* edited by Hubert Jedin and John Dolan. Augustine, however, always intended a work of moderate size, and that is precisely what *enchiridion* meant to him, as we have already seen.

Having said this, we can take a look at Augustine's discussion of faith. The whole of it may be outlined as follows, using as headings the articles of the Creed — in this case combining elements of the creeds of Hippo and Milan:

I. I believe in God the Father almighty, creator of all things, king of the ages, immortal and invisible (III, IX, 32).

> a. There are many things that a Christian need not know, but what a Christian must know is that the Triune God is the creator of all things (III, 9; also V, 16). The theme of what should be known and what need not be known is an Augustinian commonplace.[8] It is noteworthy that Augustine attributes creation to the Trinity as a whole rather than just to the Father, although the Creed itself seems to specify the Father as creator. This is Augustine's constant teaching.[9]

> b. What God created is good, although all things "are not supremely, equally or unchangeably good" (III, 10-4, IV, 15). While affirming the goodness of creation, Augustine also finds a place for evil. This section recalls the arguments to be found, for example, in the anti-Manichean work *The Nature of Good*.

> c. Although there are things that a Christian need not know, he should nonetheless shun error, which Augustine distinguishes from ignorance (V, 16-17).

> d. Lying, which is different from error, must absolutely be avoided (V, 17-VII, 22). Augustine ap-

pears to be the source of the Latin tradition that under no circumstances, except jestingly, may a lie be told.[10] In the course of this discussion Augustine addresses the skepticism of the Academics, against whom he had produced the *Answer to the Academics* soon after his conversion.

e. Angels and human beings fell of their own accord and can only be saved by the grace of God (VIII, 23-IX, 32). Augustine is the great theologian of the fall and, like many other Fathers, he is as interested in the fall of the angels as he is in that of Adam and Eve and their progeny.[11] He is also, of course, the great theologian of grace, and an insistence on the indispensability of grace and its pre-eminence vis-à-vis the human will permeates this section. This emphasis reflects Augustine's struggle with the Pelagians, for whom human endeavor was at least as important as, if not more so than, divine assistance. In this section, in VIII, 27, Augustine refers to fallen humanity as "the condemned mass" (*massa damnata*);[12] it is a term that underlines the author's extreme pessimism about ungraced human nature, and it stands in contrast to the more optimistic Pelagian view. The section concludes with a treatment of the nature of true freedom and of the relationship between grace and the will.

II. And in Jesus Christ, his only Son, our Lord . . . (X, 33-XV, 55).

a. A mediator was needed to save the fallen human race (X, 33-XIV, 55). The Word of God became incarnate and "was born of the Holy Spirit and the

Virgin Mary" in order to reconcile human beings to the Father. Christ, "one person, Word and man," is in his manhood, which is gratuitously united to the Godhead, the most striking example of unmerited grace. Although not the son of the Holy Spirit, he is born of the Spirit, which signifies his immeasurable grace. Conceived without concupiscence because he is born of a virgin, he is therefore without original sin, since Augustine asserts that original sin is passed on by way of the concupiscence that attends sexual intercourse.[13]

b. Baptism is a sharing in Christ's grace and hence a death to sin (XIII, 42-XV, 52). Augustine stresses the necessity of baptism in the face of original sin, even for newborn infants. In XXIII, 93 he teaches the damnation of unbaptized infants, although it will be "the gentlest punishment of all." This famous opinion[14] was controversial in Augustine's own day and was later rejected by the Church.

c. What Christ did in the past serves as a model for human behavior, but not what he will do in the future (XIV, 53-55).

III. And in the Holy Spirit, the Holy Church (XV, 56-16.64).

a. Belief in the Spirit, particularly as creator rather than creature, is affirmed (XV, 56). Augustine hardly dwells on the Spirit here, but he is mentioned sporadically elsewhere in the treatise, especially in XI, 37-XII, 40.

b. Profession of belief in the Church logically follows profession of belief in the Trinity; the Church exists both on earth and in heaven (XV, 56-XVI, 63). The angels, with whom Augustine deals extensively here, were of abiding interest to him, as can be seen in the treatment that he accords them.[15]

IV. The forgiveness of sins (XVII, 64-XXII, 83).

a. Forgiveness of sin is necessary in the Church on earth, and all sins can be forgiven (XVII, 64-65). A failure to believe that all sins could be forgiven in the Church (see also XXII, 83) was undoubtedly far less a characteristic of Augustine's time than of Tertullian's, some two hundred years before.[16]

b. There is forgiveness of sin on account of future judgment (XVII, 66).

c. Faith alone is insufficient for salvation; it must be accompanied by works (XVIII, 67).

d. Purification for attachments to things other than Christ must occur in this life or the next (XVII, 68-69). XVIII, 69 speaks of an *ignem quemdam purgatorium* ("a [kind of] purifying fire"). The fire need not be taken literally, but Augustine clearly intends to say that some sort of purification can occur after death, which we have come to know as purgatory. Augustine was by no means the first to suggest the existence of purgatory, but he elaborates it.[17] Prayers for the dead, part of the regular practice of the Church that is referred to in XXIX, 110, imply the existence of such a state and the possibility of a mitigated process of purification.

e. Sins may be forgiven in various ways, among which almsgiving is particularly efficacious (XIX, 70-XX, 77). Augustine, like other Fathers, understands almsgiving far more broadly than as merely the giving of money to the poor.

f. Sins may be graded as to their seriousness, and this seriousness is determined by God (XXI, 78-80). Augustine avers that some sins, such as marital intercourse solely for the sake of pleasure, are even allowed by way of apostolic concession. He concludes with the acute observation that serious sins appear small or non-existent when they are repeated often enough.

g. Sin is committed through ignorance or weakness, and through weakness the sacrament of penance is often omitted (XXII, 81-82).

h. The unforgivable sin against the Holy Spirit is the refusal to believe that sins can be forgiven in the Church (XXII, 83). Augustine addresses the notoriously controverted question about the nature of the sin against the Holy Spirit in Sermon 71, which he refers to here as "a small book."

V. The resurrection of the flesh (XXIII, 84-XXIX, 113).

a. In the resurrection to eternal life God will form glorious bodies from the elements of the bodies of the dead (XXIII, 84-91). This issue is also treated at length in *The City of God* XXII, 12-21.

b. The bodily condition of the damned, however, is a matter of little concern (XXIII, 92).

c. Neither bodily death nor damnation would have befallen human beings had there been no sin (XXIII).

d. Why some are saved and others damned belongs to the mystery of God's mercy and judgment (XXIV, 94-XXVIII, 108). No part of the *Enchiridion* is more typically Augustinian than this one, in which the author ponders the mystery of God's will in relation to human affairs. The fundamental idea here is that the divine will is utterly righteous and never thwarted by human resistance to it. Its righteousness is revealed in both salvation and damnation: salvation manifests the divine mercy, or grace, damnation the divine justice. In fact, however, although God *desires everyone to be saved* (1 Tm 2:4), most are damned, according to Augustine. Still God's desire for universal salvation is not impeded inasmuch as, even though each individual may not be saved, individuals from each class of humankind are — *kings and private citizens, nobles and commoners, important people and humble ones. . . .* This interpretation of 1 Timothy 2:4 is clearly unsatisfactory, and at the bottom of it lies Augustine's relentless pessimism about the number of the saved, the fewness of whom he accepts as a given. The section concludes with a kind of appendix on freedom of the will both before and after the fall, and on the need of a mediator after the fall.

e. Between a person's death and the final resurrection the soul abides in an appropriate place (XXIX, 109-110). Augustine does not touch on the difficult question of the nature of the intermediate state between death and final resurrection. In any event, depending on the condition of the soul of the deceased, the prayers of the living, particularly the eucharist ("the sacrifice of the mediator"), may or may not be helpful.

f. After the final resurrection there will be two cities, one of the Church and the other of the devil (XXIX, 111-113). The theme of the two cities appears many times in Augustine's writings in some form or other, not only in *The City of God*.[18] Augustine spends more time here on the sufferings of the damned than on the beatitude of the redeemed. Although he insists that their torments are eternal, an idea to which he devotes most of *The City of God* XXI, he allows for an occasional mitigation of their sufferings, which represents the reversal of a previous opinion, as stated in the *Expositions of the Psalms* 105, 2.

With that the treatment of faith concludes, and Augustine continues on to the virtue of hope, which he notes arises from faith (XXX, 114).

If the Creed serves as the basis for Augustine's reflection on faith, the Lord's Prayer acts in this capacity for his discussion on hope. The seven petitions of the Prayer, as Matthew records it, each express something to be hoped for. The first three touch upon things that begin on earth but will endure eternally in the life to come — the hallowing of God's name, the advent of his kingdom, the carrying out of his will. The remaining four — the obtaining of daily bread, the forgiveness of debts, being freed from trial and being rescued from the evil one — have to do with the needs of this life (XXX, 115). Finally, Augustine shows that Luke's shorter version of the Prayer is a complement to Matthew's in that it assists in the understanding of Matthew's (XXX, 116).

This was not the first time that Augustine had commented on the Lord's Prayer. He had already given an important account of it in his treatise *The Lord's Sermon on the Mount*, composed toward the end of the fourth century. There too, in II, 11, 38, he finds in the seven petitions of the Matthean version a combining of eternal and temporal concerns along the lines that we have seen in the *Enchiridion*. The same theme is taken up as well in some homilies in which he interprets the Prayer to a group of catechumens.[19]

At last Augustine arrives at the virtue of love, "which . . . is greater than the other two, that is faith and hope" (XXXI, 117). The few pages that Augustine devotes to love are, in their way, more sweeping than the many that he gives over to faith.

In a kind of complement to II, 7-8, he begins by discussing the relationship of the three virtues to each other and finds the true meaning of the first two in the third. Without love, the law is merely a reproach, and "the cupidity of the flesh reigns" (*ibid.*). This assertion gives Augustine an opportunity in XXXI, 118 to offer a brief theology of both individual spiritual growth and the whole of human history, each of which can be characterized by four states — the first being "according to the flesh" (*secundum carnem*) or "before the law" (*ante legem*); the second "under the law" (*sub lege*), when knowledge of sin leads to slavery to sin; the third "under grace" (*sub gratia*), when the possibility of being freed from this slavery is made available through the grace of Christ; and the fourth "in full and perfect peace" (*in pace plena et perfecta*). Historically, the state *ante legem* existed between Adam and Moses, the state *sub lege* between Moses and Christ, and the state *sub gratia* since the coming of

Christ. The fourth state is in fact eternal life. One is re-
minded of the immense view of history that climaxes *The
City of God*, in XXII, 30, starting with Adam and opening up
to (rather than ending with) the eternal day of the Lord —
all of which is compressed in as small a space as that in
which Augustine discusses the four stages from *ante legem* to
in pace in the *Enchiridion*.

After a few lines about baptism (in which, in XXXI, 119,
Augustine seems to slip by implying that baptism could be
received *in pace*), the treatise reaches its culmination in
XXXII, 121. Here Augustine affirms that love is the end of
the commandments, and he cites the two great commandments of love of God and neighbor.[20] From *Teaching Christianity* I, 35, 39-40, 44 in particular we know the central importance that he attached to these commandments, to
which he believed that all of scripture could be reduced and
in the light of which he taught that all of scripture could be
interpreted. Augustine then speaks about the workings of
love through faith in this life but face to face (*per speciem*)
with God in the next, appropriately reprising at the end of
his book something that he had said very close to the beginning of it: "When a mind is filled with the beginning of that
faith which works through love, it progresses by a good life
even toward vision (*etiam ad speciem*) . . . " (I, 5). And once
one has arrived at the vision of God and also at a perfect
comprehension of one's neighbor, and once cupidity with
its limiting power has been abolished, there will be nothing
to impede the expansion of love, and it will blossom without hindrance.

At that, with a few courteous words to Laurence in
XXXII, 122, Augustine brings his treatise to a close.

Given the exalted theological authority that Augustine
has enjoyed in the Western Church since his own lifetime,
and given the impressive scope of the *Enchiridion*, there re-

mains but one thing to point out to the reader of the present treatise, which it is hoped will make the great theologian that much more sympathetic and approachable. The reader will notice that Augustine is absolutely sure about any number of things — for some of which, like the fewness of the redeemed, he might have benefitted from an injection of doubt. But he is not sure about everything. Or, at least, there are matters that he confronts with a genuine openness. Should certain errors be categorized as sins? He does not know, and leaves the question unanswered (VII, 20). To what extent the sins of one's ancestors affect a person he likewise does not know, and he suggests that a more careful search of scripture than he has been able to carry out might yield an answer (XIII, 47). He is ignorant, too, regarding the nature of the distinctions that are said to exist among the angels; of whether the sun, the moon, and the other stars should be counted as angels (as great a Christian thinker as Origen had taken it for granted that they were rational beings[21]); and concerning the precise form in which angels have appeared to human beings (XV, 58-59). And he doubts whether anyone can know exactly when human life begins in the womb (XXIII, 86). These confessions of ignorance, made in the evening of a long life devoted in large part to the loftiest theological speculation, are the tokens of a real humility, which is itself the mark of a certain grandeur of soul and an indispensable requirement in the pursuit of truth, and they help to draw Augustine a little closer to his readers.

Boniface Ramsey, O.P.

Notes

1. See *Teaching Christianity* II, 2, 7, 9, 11; *The Trinity* XIII, 19, 24.
2. See Letter 118, 1, 21.
3. See also *Enchiridion* I, 4, 6; 33, 122.
4. See *Enchiridion* I, 2, 4, 6; VIII, 23; XII, 38.
5. The creeds in question can be found in J.N.D. Kelly, *Early Christian Creeds*, 3rd ed. (New York, 1972) 173, 176.
6. See *ibid.* 773, where the original Latin text is given.
7. See *Enchiridion* IV, 15; XIX, 74, and XXI, 79.
8. See *Confessions* V, 4, 7; *Teaching Christianity* II, 39.58-42.63.
9. See *Literal Meaning of Genesis* IX, 15, 26.
10. See *Lying* and *Against Lying*.
11. See *The City of God* XI, 11.
12. See *Enchiridion* XXIII, 92; XXV, 99; XXVIII, 107.
13. See *Marriage and Concupiscence* I, 23, 26-24, 27.
14. See *The Merits and Forgiveness of Sins* I, 27, 40; *The Soul and Its Origin* I, 9, 10.
15. See *The Literal Meaning of Genesis* IV, 28, 45-32, 50; XI, 17, 22-22, 29; *The City of God* XI.
16. See Tertullian, *De pudicitia* 19.
17. See *The City of God* XXI, 13.
18. See *Instruction of Beginners* XXI, 37; *Expositions of the Psalms* 61, 6.
19. See Sermons 56, 13, 19; 57, 6, 6-7, 7; 58, 9, 12; 59, 5, 8.
20. See Mt 22:37-40.
21. See Origen, *De principiis* I, 7, 2-5.

Editor's Note

The divisions of *The Enchiridion* are based on the studies of several prominent scholars of Augustine so I used them for the sake of clarity. The subheads are not contained in the original text. They are provided for the convenience of the reader.

The Enchiridion On Faith, Hope, and Love

Prologue

The beauty of wisdom

1,1. My dearest son Laurence, it would be impossible to say how much your learning delights me, and how much I desire that you should be wise, rather than one of those of whom scripture says *Where is the one who is wise? Where is the scribe? Where is the debater of this age? Has not God made foolish the wisdom of the world?* (1 Cor 1:20), but rather one of those of whom it is written *The multitude of the wise is the salvation of the world* (Wis 6:24). This is the kind of person the apostle wants people to be when he says to them *I want you to be wise in what is good and guileless in what is evil* (Rom 16:19).[1]

Wisdom is the same as piety

2. Now, for human beings, wisdom is the same as piety. You can read this in the book of the holy man Job. There we find that Wisdom herself said to a man *Behold, piety is wisdom* (Jb 28:28). If you ask what kind of piety she was speaking of in that place, you will find that the Greek expresses it more clearly as *theosebeia*, which is reverence toward God. There is another word for piety in Greek, *eusebeia*, which means "good reverence," although this chiefly signifies the worship of God. But no word is more suitable to explain what human wisdom is than the one that expressly denotes worship of God. You ask me to speak briefly about great

33

matters. Do you wish me to find an even conciser expression than this? Perhaps this is exactly what you wish me to explain briefly and to sum up in a few words: how God is to be worshiped.

God is to be worshiped with faith, hope, and love

3. If I answer that God is to be worshiped with faith, hope and love, you will certainly say that this is a shorter answer than you wish for, and then you will ask for a brief explanation of the objects of each of these three, that is, what we should believe, what we should hope for, and what we should love. When I have done this, you will have an answer to all the questions you put in your letter: if you have a copy of it at hand, you can easily turn to them and read them again; if not, let me help you to remember them.

The origin of the handbook

4. You write that you wish me to make a book for you to keep, what is known as a handbook, never to be let out of your hands, containing an exposition of what you have asked about, namely, what we should seek above all, what we should chiefly seek to avoid because of the various heresies there are, to what extent reason comes to the support of religion, what lies outside the scope of reason and belongs to faith alone, what should be held first and last, what the whole body of doctrine amounts to, and what is a sure and suitable foundation of Catholic faith.

Without a doubt you will know all these things for which you are looking if you take care to know what should be believed, hoped for, and loved. These are the most important things, or rather the only things, that are to be followed in religion: anybody who denies these things is either a total stranger to the name of Christ or else a heretic. These are the truths we should defend by reason, whether we know them from our bodily senses or have discovered them with the understanding of our minds. But the things that we have not discovered through sense-experience, and have been and are unable to reach with our minds, must be believed in without any doubt on the evidence of the witnesses by whom those writings that have already gained the name of sacred scripture were compiled: they were able to see these things, or even to foresee them, either physically or in their minds with divine help.

Beginning with faith and ending with vision

5. When a mind is filled with the beginning of that faith which works through love,[2] it progresses by a good life even toward vision, in which holy and perfect hearts know that unspeakable beauty the full vision of which is the highest happiness. This is without doubt what you are seeking, what we must hold first and last, beginning with faith and ending with vision. This is what the whole body of doctrine amounts to. The sure and proper foundation of the Catholic faith is Christ, as the apostle says, *For no one can lay any foundation other than the one that has been laid; that foundation is Jesus Christ* (1 Cor 3:11). Nor is the fact that this may be thought something we hold in common with some heretics any reason for denying that this is the true foundation of the Catholic faith. For if we consider carefully the things that concern Christ, Christ is found only in name among some heretics who wish to be called Christians, but in truth he is not to be found among them. To demonstrate this would take too long, since it would involve mentioning all

the heresies that have been or are or may have been under the name of Christian, and explaining how this is true in each case: such an argument would take up so many books that it would seem endless.

Your heart must be set on fire with great love

6. But what you are asking from me is a handbook, one that can be carried in the hand, not one to burden book-shelves. So let us return to the three things by which we have said God must be worshiped, faith, hope, and love: it is easy to say what must be believed, what hoped, what loved. But to defend this against the criticism of those who hold a different opinion demands fuller and more laborious teaching: for this it is necessary, not that your hand be filled with a brief handbook, but that your heart be set on fire with great love.

The Creed and the Lord's Prayer

2, 7. Think of the Creed and the Lord's Prayer. What text is there that takes a shorter time to hear or to read? What is there that is easier to commit to memory? Because the human race was oppressed with great misery because of sin, and stood in need of the divine mercy, the prophet foretold the time of God's grace and said *Then everyone who calls on the name of the Lord shall be saved* (Jl 2:32).[3] That is the reason for the prayer. But when the apostle quoted this testimony of the prophet in order actually to proclaim God's grace, he immediately added *But how are they to call on one in whom they have not believed?* (Rom 10:14). That is why we have the Creed. Notice that the three things we mentioned earlier are contained in these two: faith believes, hope and love pray. But hope and love cannot be without faith, and so faith prays as well. That is why Paul said *But how are they to call on one in whom they have not believed?*

Love cannot exist without hope nor hope without love, nor can either exist without faith

8. What is there that we can hope for without believing in it? To be sure, we can believe in things for which we do not hope. Who among the faithful does not believe in the punishments of the wicked, but without hoping for them? Anybody who believes they are destined for him, and in his mind runs away from them in horror, is more rightly said to fear them than to hope for them. One writer has written to distinguish the two

Give hope to the fearful.[4]

Another, though a better poet, speaks inaccurately when he says:

Had I been able to hope for this one sorrow.[5]

Some teachers of grammar use this line as an example to illustrate the improper use of words and comment "he said 'hope' instead of 'fear'." So there is faith in good things and bad, for both good and bad things are believed, and both in good faith, not bad. There is also faith in past realities, in present ones, and in future ones. We believe that Christ died, which is now in the past; we believe that he sits at the right hand of the Father, which is in the present; we believe that he will come in judgment, which is in the future. There is also faith in things that concern us, and in things that concern others; everybody believes that he had a beginning, that he has not always existed, and that the same is true of other people and other things. We have also many religious beliefs not only concerning other humans, but also concerning angels.

But hope is only for good things, only for things that are in the future and concern the one who is said to have hope in them. For these reasons it has been necessary to make a rational distinction between faith and hope and to give them different names. The fact that we do not see either the things we believe in or those we hope for makes not seeing a feature that faith and hope have in common. In the Letter to the Hebrews, on whose testimony distinguished defenders of Catholic faith and discipline[6] have relied, faith is said to be *the conviction of things not seen* (Heb 11:1). However, if a person asserts that he has believed (that is, he has found faith), not in words, not in witnesses, not in arguments of any kind, but in the evidence of things actually present to him, we do not think him so absurd that it would be right to criticize his expression and say to him "you have seen, and therefore you have not believed"; so it may be thought not to follow that something that is believed is not necessarily unseen. But it is better to follow the teaching of the divine words in reserving the name of "faith" for faith in things that are not seen. The apostle also speaks of hope, saying *Now hope that is seen is not hope. For who hopes for what is seen? But if we hope for what we do not see, we wait for it with patience* (Rom 8:24-25). So when we believe that good things await us in the future, this is nothing other than to hope for them. And now what should I say about love? Without it faith has no value. But hope cannot exist without love. The apostle James says *Even the demons believe—and shudder* (Jas 2:19), yet they do not hope or love, but rather fear that which we hope for and love, believing that it will come about. That is why the apostle Paul approves and recommends *the faith that works through love* (Gal 5:6), which cannot exist without hope. So love cannot exist without hope nor hope without love, nor can either exist without faith.

Faith in God the Creator

The cause of created things is the goodness of the creator

3, 9. Since, therefore, we are considering what ought to be believed in the sphere of religion, we do not need to inquire into the nature of things as did those whom the Greeks call "phusikoi," nor need we fear that the Christian is ignorant of something he discovered or think he has discovered considering the properties and number of the elements, the movement and order and phases of the stars, the shape of the heavens, the kinds of animals, fruits, stones, springs, rivers, and mountains and their natures, the measurement of time and space, the indications of imminent storms and hundreds of other such things. This is because they themselves have not discovered everything, powerful as they are of intellect, eager in study, and abundantly gifted with leisure: some matters they investigate with the power of human speculation, others on the basis of facts and experience, and in those matters which they boast of having discovered much is a matter of opinion rather than knowledge. For a Christian it is enough to believe that the cause of created things, whether in heaven or on earth, visible or invisible, is nothing other than the goodness of the creator who is the one true God, and that there is nothing that is not either himself or from him, and that he is Trinity, that is, Father, the Son begotten from the Father and the Holy Spirit who proceeds from the same Father,[7] and is one and the same Spirit of Father and Son.

10. By this Trinity, supremely, equally, and unchange-ably good, all things have been created: they are not su-premely, equally, or unchangeably good, but even when they are considered individually, each one of them is good; and at the same time all things are very good, since in all these things consists the wonderful beauty of the universe.

Evil is the removal of good

11. In this universe even that which is called evil, well or-dered, and kept in its place, sets the good in higher relief, so that good things are more pleasing and praiseworthy than evil ones. Nor would Almighty God, "to whom," as even the pagans confess, "belongs supreme power,"[8] since he is su-premely good, in any way allow anything evil to exist among his works were he not so omnipotent and good that he can bring good even out of evil. For what else is that which is called evil but a removal of good? In the bodies of animals, to be afflicted with diseases and wounds is nothing other than to be deprived of health: the aim of treatment is not to make the evils which were in the body, such as dis-eases and wounds, move from where they were to some-where else, but rather that they should cease to exist, since a wound or a disease is not in itself a substance but a defect in the substance of flesh. The flesh itself is the substance, a good thing to which those evil things, those removals of the good, known as health, occur. In the same way all evils that affect the mind are removals of natural goods: when they are cured they are not moved to somewhere else, but when they are no longer in the mind once it has been restored to health, they will be nowhere.

Corruption cannot consume good without consuming the thing itself

4, 12. So all are good, since the maker of all beings is supremely good. But since they are not supremely and unchangeably good like their creator, in them goodness can be decreased and increased. For good to be decreased is evil, even though, however much it is decreased, some of it must remain for the being to exist at all, if it does still exist. Nor can the good that makes it a thing entirely cease to be, however small the thing is and of whatever kind, unless the thing itself ceases to be as well. Rightly a being that is not corrupted is highly esteemed; furthermore, if it is incorruptible, completely incapable of corruption, it is worthy of still higher esteem. But when it is corrupted, its corruption is an evil because it deprives it of some good. If it did not deprive it of good, it would not harm it; but it does harm it, and therefore it takes away good. So for as long as a being is corrupted, there still remains in it some good that can be removed, and so if in a being there remains something that cannot be corrupted, such a thing will be incorruptible, and will arrive at this state, which is so good, by way of corruption. But if it never ceases to be corrupted, it will never cease to contain some good that corruption can remove from it. If corruption totally consumes it, no good will remain in it, for it will have ceased to exist. So corruption cannot consume good without consuming the thing itself. Therefore every being is good, a great good if it cannot be corrupted, a small one if it can: but it cannot be denied, except by fools and the inexpert, that it is good. If it is consumed by corruption, then corruption itself will no longer exist, since there will be no being for it to exist in.

Good and evil people

13. From this it follows that if there were nothing good, there would be nothing that could be called bad. But good that is without any evil is wholly good, while good that has evil in it is a contaminated or corrupt good. Nor can there ever be any evil where there is no good. This leads to a surprising conclusion, which is that since every being insofar as it exists is good, when we speak of a contaminated thing as evil, we are saying nothing other than that something good is bad, and that only what is good is bad: since every being is a good thing, nor would there be any evil thing if the very thing that is evil were not a being. So only something good can be evil. When this is said it seems absurd, and yet this line of thinking leads inevitably to this conclusion. We must beware lest we incur the censure of the prophecy in which we read *Woe to those who call evil good and good evil, who say darkness for light and light for darkness, who say bitter for sweet and sweet for bitter!* (Is 5:20). And the Lord himself says *The evil person out of evil treasure of the heart produces evil* (Lk 6:45).[9] But what is an evil man if not an evil being, since a man is a being? Moreover, if a man is something good because he is a being, what is an evil man but an evil good? But when we make a distinction we find that he is not an evil because he is a man, nor is he a good because he is wicked, but he is a good because he is a man and an evil because he is wicked. So whoever says "It is evil to be a man" or "it is good to be wicked," he incurs the censure of the prophet *Woe to those who call evil good and good evil,* for he speaks ill of God's work, which is the man, and praises man's vice, which is that man's iniquity. So every being, even if it is corrupt, insofar as it is a being is good, and insofar as it is corrupt, is evil.

Two contraries cannot exist simultaneously in one thing

14. So with regard to those two opposites that are called good and evil, the rule of the logicians fails according to which they say that two contraries cannot exist simultaneously in one thing. For no air is simultaneously dark and light, no food or drink is simultaneously sweet and sour, no body is simultaneously black and white in the same place, or ugly and beautiful in the same place. We find this to be true in many, indeed in almost all contraries, that they cannot coexist in one thing simultaneously. But while nobody doubts that good and evil are contraries, not only can they exist simultaneously, but evils cannot exist at all without goods, and they can only exist in goods, although goods can exist without evils. For a man or an angel is capable of not being unjust, but someone who is unjust can only be either a man or an angel: that he is a man or an angel is a good, while that he is unjust is an evil. And these two contraries coexist in such a way that evil would be quite unable to exist if there were no good for it to exist in, since not only would corruption have nowhere to be, but it would have nowhere to arise from if there were nothing to be corrupted, since only a good thing can be corrupted, corruption being the extermination of good. So evils have arisen out of goods, and they only exist within things that are in some way good. There was nowhere else for any evil being to arise from. If there were, it would plainly be good insofar as it was a being, and either it would be that great good which is an incorruptible being, or else corruptible nature would in no way exist were it not in some way a good, which corruption was able to spoil by corrupting what was good.

The tree and the fruits

15. But while we have said that evils arise out of goods, we should not be thought to be contradicting the saying of the Lord *A good tree cannot bear bad fruit* (Mt 7:18). For, as Truth has said, grapes cannot be gathered from thorns, because grapes cannot grow from thorns; but we see that both vines and thornbushes can grow from good soil. In the same way an evil will, like an evil tree, cannot make good fruits, that is, good works, but from the good nature of man both a good and an evil will can arise.[10] Nor was there anything at all for evil will to arise from at the beginning except the good nature of angels and men. The Lord demonstrates this most clearly in the place where he was speaking about the tree and the fruits. He says *Either make the tree good, and its fruit good; or make the tree bad, and its fruit bad* (Mt 12:33). Here he warns us with sufficient clarity that evil fruits cannot grow from a good tree or good fruits from an evil tree, but that from the earth itself, to which he was speaking, both kinds of tree can grow.

5, 16. This being so, although we love the line of Vergil that says

> Happy was he who was able to know the causes of things[11]

it does not seem to us to have anything to do with the pursuit of happiness if we know the causes of the great movements of physical objects in the world, which are hidden away in the most secret extremities of the natural universe:

> Whence come the tremblings of the earth,
> what power causes the deep seas to swell and break
>   their bounds,
> and then to subside into themselves again[12]

and suchlike. But we must know the causes of good and evil things insofar as it is allowed to man to know them in this life which is so full of errors and troubles, in order that he may avoid those same errors and troubles. What we must do, surely, is make our way toward that happiness where we shall not be disturbed by any trouble or deceived by any error. If we were obliged to know the causes of the movements of physical objects, there would be nothing more necessary for us to know than the causes of our own health; but since we seek out physicians in our ignorance of them, who cannot see with what great patience we should bear our ignorance of the secrets of the heavens and the earth?

Error: One takes something false to be true

17. For although we should beware of error with all possible care, not only in great matters but also in lesser ones, and although the only possible cause of error is ignorance, it does not follow that anybody who is ignorant of something is thereby in error, but only a person who thinks he knows what he does not know: he takes something false to be true, and that is exactly what error consists in. What is most important is what a person is in error about. For in a single matter one who knows is rightly preferred to one who does not know and one who is not in error to one who is. But in different matters, that is, when one person knows some things and another others, one knowing useful things and another useless or even harmful things, with regard to these latter things, who would not put the one who does not know them above the one who does? For there are some things of which ignorance is better than knowledge.

Also, there have been times when to err has been advantageous to some people, but only on paths we travel with our feet, not on the path of the moral life. It has happened to me myself that I lost my way[13] at a crossroads and so did not pass through a place where I would have been ambushed by an armed band of Donatists[14] had they discovered me traveling there, and so it happened that I arrived at my destination by a circuitous route, and when I discovered they had laid an ambush I was glad that I had lost my way and gave thanks for this to God. Who would hesitate to set a traveler who lost his way like that above a robber who did not lose his way? Perhaps that is why in the works of the same supreme poet some unhappy lover says:

> How I saw, how I perished, how my evil error took
>   me away![15]

since there is also a good kind of error which not only does me no harm but even brings me some good.

But if we consider the truth more carefully, it seems that to err is nothing other than to think true what is false and to think false what is true, to think what is certain uncertain or what is uncertain certain, whether it is false or true, and since this is an ugliness and deformity in the mind equal to the beauty and suitability we perceive in the words *yes, yes; no, no* (Mt 5:37) when a person speaks or gives assent. Indeed, this is certainly one reason why the life we lead is a miserable one, that from time to time error is necessary to preserve life. Far otherwise is that life in which Truth itself is the life of our soul, in which nobody deceives or is deceived. But here men deceive and are deceived, and they are more to be pitied when they deceive by lying than when they themselves are deceived by putting trust in liars. So much does our rational nature flee falsehood and avoid error as much as it can, that even those who love to deceive are unwilling to be deceived. For a liar does not think he is in error himself, but rather that he is causing another who believes him to err. And indeed in that respect he is not in

error, but rather concealing the truth, if he himself knows
what is true, but he is deceived in thinking that his lie does
him no harm, since sin is always more harmful to the person
who commits it than to the one who suffers it.

Lying

6, 18. But here a very difficult and complicated question
arises, about which I have already written a large book[16]
when obliged to reply to the question whether it was ever
the duty of a just man to lie. For there are some people who
have gone so far as to claim that it is sometimes a good and
religious thing to commit perjury and to speak falsely about
things that concern the worship of God and even the very
nature of God himself.

But my view is that all lying is sin, but that it is very significant with what intention and about what matters a person lies. For a person who lies with the intention of helping
somebody does not sin in the same way as one who lies with
the intention of doing harm, nor does a person who sends a
traveler on a different route by lying do as much harm as
one who by lying deceives another and leads him to take an
evil path in life.

Certainly, nobody is to be judged a liar who says something false while believing it to be true, since as far as he is
concerned he is not deceiving but deceived. Nor is a person
to be accused of lying, but rather of rashness, who considers
true false things in which he has placed his belief too incautiously: on the contrary, insofar as the person himself is
concerned, the person who deserves the title of liar more is
the one who says something true which he believes to be
false. For as far as his mind is concerned, since he does not
believe what he says, he does not speak the truth, although

what he says may be discovered to be true; nor is a person at all free from the sin of lying who unknowingly speaks the truth with his mouth while his conscious will is to tell a lie.

If we do not consider the subject matter about which a person is speaking, but only the intention of the speaker, a person who unknowingly tells an untruth because he believes it to be true is better than one who knowingly has the disposition of a liar and does not know that what he is saying is true. In the former person the mind and the words are consistent while the other, whatever the nature of what he says in itself, has one thought hidden in his breast and another ready on his tongue, and this is the evil proper to the liar.

But with regard to the words that are spoken, it is very important to consider the subject matter about which a person is deceived or lies, so that, while to be deceived is a lesser evil than to lie insofar as a person's will is concerned, it is very much more tolerable to lie in matters not concerned with religion than to be deceived in matters of faith in which or knowledge of which is necessary for the worship of God. To illustrate this by examples, let us compare the case of a person who lies by announcing that somebody is dead with that of one who mistakenly believes that Christ will die again, however long this death may be delayed: is it not far better to lie in the former way than to be deceived in the latter, and a much lesser evil to lead a person into the former error than to be led by someone else into the latter?

Every error is in itself an evil

19. In some matters we are deceived by a great evil, in others by a little one, in others by no evil at all, and in some matters we are even deceived by some good. A man is de-

ceived by a great evil when he does not believe what leads to eternal life or believes something that leads to eternal death, but he is deceived by a small one when, taking the false to be true, he falls into some temporal difficulties such as a faithful person can turn to good use by his patience: for example, when somebody, thinking a person to be good who is in fact evil, suffers some evil from him.

But someone who believes an evil person to be good without suffering any evil from him is not deceived by any evil, and so does not bring on himself the scorn of the prophet who says *woe to those who call evil good* (Is 5:20). These words should be understood as spoken about the things that make people evil, not about people themselves. So a person who says that adultery is good rightly comes under the censure of these words of the prophet; but a person who calls somebody good, thinking him to be chaste and not knowing that he is an adulterer, is not deceived by false doctrine concerning what is good and evil, but concerning secrets of human behavior, calling a person good whom he believes to be that which he knows to be good, and calling an adulterer evil and a chaste person good, but calling this person good without knowing that he is an adulterer and not chaste. Furthermore, if a person escapes danger through an error, as I said earlier had happened to me when I was on a journey, even something good comes to that person by reason of his error.

But when I say that in some cases it is not evil, or is even in some way good, to be deceived, I am not saying that error itself is not an evil or is in some way good, but I am speaking about the evil that is avoided or the good that is arrived at by way of error, that is, the evil that does not happen or the advantage that comes about because of the error. For error in itself in an important matter is a great evil and in a small matter a small evil, but it is always an evil. For who without error can deny that it is evil to take the false for true or to deny the truth as false, or to consider uncertain what is certain or certain what is uncertain? It is one thing to believe that an evil man is good, which is an error, and another to suffer no evil from the evil of that error, when an evil man who is thought to be good does no harm. Similarly, it is one thing to think a particular way is the right way when it is not, and another to receive some good, such as escaping an ambush of evil men, from that error which is in itself evil.

Every error is not a sin

7, 20. I really do not know about other errors such as these: when a person thinks well of an evil person, not knowing what he is like, or when similar things happen regarding what we perceive through our bodily senses, so that we perceive things spiritually as if we were perceiving them physically or physically as if we were perceiving them spiritually (like the apostle Peter when he thought he was seeing a vision when he was suddenly freed from bondage and imprisonment by an angel),[17] or when with regard to physical things we think something is smooth when in fact it is rough, or sweet when it is bitter or sweetly perfumed when it has a foul smell, or when we mistake the noise of a chariot passing for thunder, or when we mistake one person for another very like him, as happens often in the case of twins (so that Vergil says

And the error was pleasing to their parents[18]):

I do not know whether these and other similar occurrences are also to be called sins.

Nor have I undertaken at this moment to unravel the complicated question which tormented Academics,[19] those sharpest of intellects, that is, whether a wise man should agree to anything, for fear of falling into error by taking the false as true since, as they assert, everything is either hidden or uncertain. For this reason I wrote three books soon after my conversion, to remove from my path the obstacle which their arguments put before me, as it were, on the threshold, and indeed it was necessary to remove that despair of finding the truth which their arguments seemed to foster.[20] According to them, then, every error is thought to be sin, which they claim can only be avoided by the avoidance of all assent. They say that anybody who assents to an uncertainty is in error, that there is nothing certain in human sight because the true and the false are so similar as to be indistinguishable, even if what is seen does happen to be true: these are their arguments, most ingenious but most shameless.

For us, however, *the righteous live by their faith* (Hb 2:4).[21] But if assent is taken away, faith is taken away, since nothing can be believed without assent. And those things that we must believe in order to come to the blessed life which can only be eternal are true, although we cannot see them. But I do not know whether we should speak with those who not only do not know that they will live eternally, but do not even know that they are alive now: indeed, they claim not to know what they cannot but know. Nor can anybody be ignorant that he is alive, since if he is not alive he is unable even to be ignorant of anything, since not only knowledge, but also ignorance, belongs to the living. Clearly, by not acknowledging that they are alive they seem to be taking care to avoid error, but their error itself proves that they are alive, since nobody who is not alive can err. So, just as it is not only true but certain that we are alive, so many other things are true and certain, and to deny this is properly known, not as wisdom, but as insanity.

Error, though not always a sin, is always an evil

21. But as for things concerning which, as far as gaining the kingdom of God is concerned, it does not matter whether we believe them or not, nor whether they are true or false, to err about such things, that is, to think one thing rather than another, should not be considered a sin, or if it is, the tiniest and least serious of sins. In the last analysis, whatever it is and however important, it has nothing to do with the path we take to God, which is the path of faith working through love.[22] The pleasing error of the parents concerning their twins did not take them away from this path; nor did the apostle Peter leave this path when, thinking he was seeing a vision, he mistook one thing for another so that the bodily images with which he thought he was surrounded prevented him from recognizing the bodily images by which he was in fact surrounded until the angel by whom he had been freed left him;[23] nor was the patriarch Jacob straying from this path when he believed that his son had been killed by a beast when he was in fact alive.[24] In these and similar mistakes we are deceived without damage to our faith in God, and we err without straying from the path that leads to him.

These errors, even if they are not sins, are nonetheless to be counted among the evils of this life, which is so subject to vanity that false things are here taken for true, the true is rejected as false, and what is uncertain is taken as certain. For although these things do not belong to that true and certain faith by which we move toward eternal happiness, they do belong to the misery in which we are still living now: we would not be deceived in any way in the perceptions of our minds or of our senses if we were already enjoying that true and perfect happiness.

To use words for deception, and not for what they were in-stituted, is a sin

22. To go further, however, every lie must be called a sin because a person, not only when he himself knows what is true but also when he errs and is deceived, being human, must say what is in his mind, whether it is true or he only thinks it true, when it is false. But everyone who lies speaks contrary to what is in his mind, with the intention of deceiving. Words were surely instituted not so that people could deceive each other with them, but so that each person could make his thoughts known to another. So to use words for deception, and not for what they were instituted, is a sin.

Nor should it be thought that any lie is not sinful because we can sometimes do a person good by lying. We can also do good by stealing, if a poor person to whom we secretly give what we have stolen feels a benefit and the rich person from whom we have secretly stolen is not aware of any loss: this would not lead anybody to say that such a theft was not sinful. We can also do good by adultery, if it seems that a woman will die from lack of love unless this is granted to her, and that if she lives she will be cleansed of her sin by penitence: this will not be thought a reason for denying that such adultery is sinful. But if we rightly love chastity, what is wrong with truth if for the good of another we will violate it by lying although we would not violate chastity by committing adultery? It cannot be denied that people who lie only for the salvation of others have made great progress in goodness; but it is the good will of those who have made such progress, not their lying, that is rightly praised and even rewarded with temporal gifts. It is enough to excuse their lying without praising it as well, especially in the case of the heirs of the new covenant, to whom these words are addressed: *Let your word be "Yes, Yes" or "No, No": anything more than this comes from the evil one* (Mt 5:37). Because of this evil one, since he never ceases to insinuate himself into our mortal affairs, the coheirs of Christ[25] say: *Forgive us our trespasses* (Mt 6:12).

Faith in Christ the Redeemer

Causes of good and evil

8, 23. Having treated these matters with the brevity that a book like this demands, since we must know the causes of good and evil insofar as is necessary to enable us to travel along the road that leads us to the kingdom where there will be life without death, truth without error, happiness without anxiety, we must in no way doubt that the only cause of the good things that come our way is the goodness of God, while the cause of our evils is the will of a changeable good falling away from the unchangeable good, first the will of an angel, then the will of a human being.

Ignorance and desire

24. This is the first evil that affected the rational creation, the first privation of good. Then there came even upon those who did not wish it ignorance of what should be done and desire for harmful things, together with their companions' error and suffering: when these two evils are felt to be near at hand, the movement of the mind fleeing them is called fear. Further, when the mind gains the things it desires, however harmful and empty they may be, since it does not realize their true nature because of its error, it is either overcome with a sick pleasure or inflated with empty joy. These are, as it were, the sources of sickness, sources

not of abundance but of deprivation, from which all the un-happiness of rational nature flows.

Death of the body

25. However, this nature, among all its evils, has not been able to lose the appetite for happiness. Rather, these evils are common to both human beings and angels who have been condemned for their malice by the Lord's justice. But man has also his own special penalty, since he has been punished with the death of the body as well. God had threatened him with the punishment of death if he sinned, bestowing free will on him while still ruling him by his authority and terrifying him with the thought of death, and placing him in the bliss of paradise as if in the shadow of life, from which he was to rise to better things if he preserved his state of justice.

Adam's sin

26. After his sin he became an exile from this place and bound also his progeny, which by his sin he had damaged within himself as though at its root,[26] by the penalty of death and condemnation. As a result, any offspring born of him and the wife through whom he had sinned, who had been condemned together with him, born through the concupiscence of the flesh which was their punishment, carrying within it a disobedience similar to that which they had showed, would contract original sin,[27] which would drag it through various errors and pains to that final punishment with the deserter angels, his corruptors, masters, and accomplices. *Therefore, sin came into the world through one man, and death came through sin, and so it spread to all: in him all have*

sinned (Rom 5:12).[28] When he used the word "world" in that text, the apostle was of course referring to the whole human race.

God judged it better to bring good out of evil than to allow nothing evil to exist

27. So that was how things stood. The condemned mass of the whole human race lay prostrate in evil, or rather was wallowing in evil and hurtling from evil to evil, and in common with those of the angels who had sinned, was paying the penalty most justly deserved by their disloyal desertion. The deeds the evil do willingly as a result of their blind and untamed concupiscence, together with their punishments, which are plain for all to see and which they suffer against their will, belong to God's just anger. But this does not mean that the goodness of the creator failed or that he ceased to bestow on the angels their life and vital powers, without which they would die, or to give form and life to the seeds of men, born though they are from corrupt and condemned stock, or to control the growth of their limbs through time and space, to give life to their senses or to feed them. He judged it better to bring good out of evil than to allow nothing evil to exist.

And if he had willed no reformation of man to bring him to a better condition, as in the case of the wicked angels, would it not have been just that the being that has deserted God, which by the evil use of its power has trampled under foot and transgressed the command of its creator, that it could very easily have kept, which has impaired the image of its maker within itself by proudly turning away from his light, which by the evil use of free choice has broken away from healthy obedience to his laws, should be eternally deserted by him and pay the eternal penalty that it has deserved? It plainly would be so, if the one who is just were not also so merciful, showing his unmerited mercy the more clearly in choosing rather to set free the unworthy.

The angels

9, 28. So after some angels in wicked pride had deserted God and been cast down into the deep darkness of the air, the remaining angels stayed in eternal happiness with God. There was not one fallen and condemned angel who had engendered the others, so that the original evil might bind them in the chains of harmful succession and drag them all to their deserved punishment, but after the one who became the devil was exalted with his companions in wickedness and was laid low with them because of this exaltation, the rest remained with the Lord in loyal obedience and also received what the others did not have, a sure knowledge to make them secure concerning their own everlasting stability from which they were never to fall.

The promise made to the saints

29. So it pleased God the maker and governor of all things that, since it was not the whole company of angels that had perished by deserting God, those who had perished should remain in perpetual perdition, while those who had persevered with God when the others deserted should have the joy of knowing that their future happiness was assured; as for the other part of the rational creation, that is humankind, since they had totally perished by reason of their sins and punishments, both original and each person's own, some of them should be restored to fill the

gap left in the company of the angels by the devil's fall. For this is the promise made to the saints when they rise again, that they will be equal to the angels of God.[29]

So the Jerusalem that is above, our mother, the city of God,[30] will not be cheated of the due number of her citizens, or perhaps will reign with an even greater number. For we do not know the number either of holy men and women, or of the impure demons into whose place will succeed the children of that holy mother who appeared barren on earth, to live unendingly in the peace from which they fell. But the number that there will be of those citizens, either now or in the future, is in the contemplation of the maker who calls into existence the things that do not exist,[31] and arranges *all things by measure and number and weight* (Wis 11:20).

By grace you have been saved through faith

30. But can this part of the human race to which God promises freedom and an eternal kingdom be rewarded for its works? Certainly not! What good can one who is ruined do, except insofar as he is set free from his ruin? Can he perhaps do good by the free choice of his own will? This too must not be thought, for it was by evil use of his power of free choice that man ruined both that power and himself. Just as a person who kills himself is alive when he does so, but by doing so becomes no longer alive, nor is he able to revive himself once he has killed himself, so when sin is committed by free choice sin is the victor and free choice also is lost, *for people are slaves to whatever masters them* (2 Pt 2:19)—this is certainly the opinion of the apostle Peter. And as it is correct, I ask what freedom can be enjoyed by one bound to slavery except when he takes pleasure in sin? One who gladly does the will of his master is serving freely,

and in this way one who is a slave of sin is free to sin. So he will not be free to act justly unless he is freed from sin and begins to be a slave of justice.

This is a true freedom because of the joy he finds in doing good, and a faithful slavery because he is doing as he has been told. But how will a person who has been sold into slavery and is bound by it find freedom to do good unless he is redeemed by the one who said *if the Son makes you free, you will be free indeed* (Jn 8:36)? Before this begins to take place in a person, how can anybody who is not yet free to do good boast of his free choice as shown in a good deed, unless he is puffed up with empty pride, against which the apostle warns when he says *by grace you have been saved through faith* (Eph 2:8).

We are truly free when God makes us

31. And lest such people claim that faith at least is their own achievement, not realizing that this has been given them by God, as the same apostle said in another place that he received mercy that he might be faithful,[32] here too he went on to add: *and this is not your own doing; it is the gift of God, not the result of works, so that no one may boast.*[33] Lest his readers might think the faithful would be lacking in good works, he further added *For we are what he has made us, created in Christ Jesus for good works, which God prepared beforehand to be our way of life.*[34] We are truly made free when God makes us, that is, forms and creates us, not that we may be men, which he has already done, but that we may be good men: this he does now by his grace, that we may be a new creation in Christ, according to the saying *Create a pure heart in me, O God* (Ps 51:10). For it could not be said that God had not al-

ready created his heart, as far as the nature of a human heart is concerned.

Give what you command; command what you will

32. Also, so that nobody, although not boasting of his works, might boast of the freedom of his will, as if he had earned as a reward the very freedom to do good works, let him hear the same proclaimer of grace saying *for it is God who is at work in you, enabling you both to will and to work for his good pleasure* (Phil 2:13), and in another place *So it comes not from the one who wills or runs, but from God who shows mercy* (Rom 9:16). Since there is no doubt whatever that a man, if he is already old enough to have the use of reason, cannot believe, hope, or love unless he wills to do so, nor can he win the reward of God's high vocation unless he runs for it willingly, how can it depend not on human will or exertion but on the God who shows mercy unless the will itself is prepared by the Lord,[35] as it is written.

Alternatively, if the words *So it comes not from the one who wills or runs, but from God who shows mercy* are written because it depends both on human will and on God's mercy, so that we should understand the text *So it comes not from the one who wills or runs, but from God who shows mercy* as if it said "human will alone is not enough without God's mercy," then God's mercy is not enough without human will; consequently, if it is right to say *So it comes not from the one who wills or runs, but from God who shows mercy* because it is not done by human will alone, why is it not right also to say the opposite, "it depends not on God who shows mercy but on human will," since it is not done by God's mercy alone? Further, since no Christian will dare to say "It depends not on God's mercy but on human will" for fear of openly contradicting the apostle, it remains for us to recognize that the words *So it comes not from the one who wills or runs, but from God who shows mercy* are said truly, that all may be given to God, who makes the good will of man ready for his help and helps the will he has made ready.

For the good will of man precedes many of God's gifts, but not all of them, and is itself one of the gifts that it does not precede. For in sacred scripture we read both *his mercy shall go before me* (Ps 59:10) and *his mercy shall follow me* (Ps 23:6): it goes before the unwilling, that they may will, and it follows the willing, that they may not will in vain. For why are we commanded to pray for our enemies[36] although they plainly have not the will to live holy lives, if not in order that God may be at work in them, enabling them to will? And why are we commanded to ask that we may receive[37] if not in order that he who has given us the will may give us that which our will desires? Let us pray, then, for our enemies, that his mercy may go before them as it has also gone before us: let us also pray for ourselves, that his mercy may follow us.

The grace of God through our Lord Jesus Christ

10, 33. So the human race was justly held in condemnation, and all its members were children of wrath. Of this wrath it is written: *For all our days have come to an end, and in your wrath we have ceased to be; our years will make designs like a spider* (Ps 90:9), and Job says of it *A mortal, born of woman, few of days and full of wrath* (Jb 14:1). And the Lord Jesus said of this wrath *Whoever believes in the Son has eternal life; whoever disobeys the Son will not see life, but God's wrath endures over him* (Jn 3:36). He does not say "God's wrath will come to him" but *God's wrath endures over him*. In fact, every human being is born with this wrath, which is why the apostle says *for we were by nature children of wrath, like everyone else* (Eph 2:3).

Since human beings were in this wrath because of original sin, which became more serious and damaging as they added more or worse sins, there was need for a mediator, that is, a reconciler, to appease this wrath by the offering of a unique sacrifice, of which all the sacrifices of the law and the prophets were shadows. Hence the apostle says *For if while we were enemies, we were reconciled to God through the death of his Son, much more surely, having been reconciled in his blood, will we be saved through him from the wrath of God* (Rom 5:10). When God is said to be angry, this does not mean that his mind was disturbed like the mind of a person who is angry, but by the application of a term used for human feelings, his vengeance, which is nothing but just, is called his anger. So our reconciliation with God by a mediator and our reception of the Holy Spirit to make us children of the one to whom we were enemies—*For all who are led by the Spirit of God are children of God* (Rom 8:14)—this is the grace of God through our Lord Jesus Christ.

Jesus born of Mary

34. About this mediator it would take a long time to say as much as deserves to be said, although in fact no man can say what deserves to be said. For who can find suitable words to explain this one truth, that *The Word became flesh and lived among us* (Jn 1:14), that we may believe in the only Son of God the almighty Father, born of the Holy Spirit and the Virgin Mary? Yet we can say that when the Word became flesh, flesh was taken by the Godhead; the Godhead was not changed into flesh. In this text by "flesh" we must understand "man," a part standing for the whole, as

when it is said *For no flesh*—that is, no man—*will be justified by the works of the law.* For it is not right to say that in that taking anything was lacking that belongs to human nature; but in this case we mean a human nature entirely free from every entanglement of sin, not of the sort that is born to the two sexes through the concupiscence of the flesh with bondage to sin, whose guilt is washed away in rebirth, but the sort that could only be born from a virgin, conceived not by desire but by the faith of his mother. But if her virginity were impaired[38] by his birth he would not then be born of a virgin, and the whole Church would be wrong—which God forbid—in acknowledging him as born of the virgin Mary, the Church which in imitation of his Mother daily brings his members to birth, and remains a virgin. Read, if you will, the letter on the virginity of holy Mary that I wrote to the illustrious Volusianus, whom I name with respect and affection.[39]

Son of God and Son of Man

35. So Christ Jesus, the Son of God, is God and man: God before all worlds, man in our world: God because he is the Word of God—for *the Word was God* (Jn 1:1)—and because a rational soul and flesh were joined to the Word in one person. Therefore insofar as he is God, he and the Father are one,[40] and insofar as he is man, the Father is greater than he.[41] But since he is the only Son of God, by nature and not by grace, he became also the Son of Man that he might also be full of grace; he, one and the same, is both, one Christ from both natures since, though he was in the form of God, he did not regard what he was by nature, that is, being equal to God, as something to be grasped. But he emptied himself, taking the form of a servant, not losing or diminishing

the form of God.[42] And through this he was both made less
and remained equal, one and the same person in each case,
as has been said. But he is different as regards the Word and
as regards man: as regards the Word he is equal, as regards
man lesser; one and the same person is Son of Man and Son
of God; there are not two sons of God, divine and human,
but one Son of God, God without beginning, man from a
certain beginning in time, our Lord Jesus Christ.

The Word is full of grace

11, 36. Here the grace of God is made clearly and abundantly plain. For what did human nature in Christ the man
do to deserve being assumed in a unique way into the unity
of the person of the one Son of God? What good will, what
care for carrying out good intentions, what good works
went before, that that man might be worthy to be one person with God? Was he human before, and was the unique
benefit offered to him alone of being worthy of God? Certainly from the moment when he began to be human he began to be nothing other than the Son, the only Son, of God,
and because of God the Word, which on assuming him became flesh, he was certainly God so that, just as any human
being is one person, that is, a rational soul and flesh, so
Christ is one person, Word and man. From where can human nature have received such great glory, which is without
doubt a free gift, given without preceding merit? Surely, to
those who consider the matter soberly and with faith, that
great grace which is God's alone is here plainly shown, that
men may understand that they are both freed from their
sins and justified by the very grace which made Christ the
man unable to have any sin. So it was that the angel greeted
his mother when he announced to her this future birth, say-

ing *Hail, full of grace* (Lk 1:28), and a little later *You have found grace with God* (Lk 1:30). Now she was indeed said to be full of grace and to have found grace with God in order that she might be the mother of her Lord, or rather of the Lord of all. But about Christ himself the evangelist John, having said *and the Word became flesh and lived among us, and we have seen*, continues *his glory, glory as of a Father's only Son, full of grace and truth* (Jn 1:14). When he says *the Word became flesh*, he means the Word is full of grace, and when he says *glory as of a Father's only Son*, he means he is full of truth. The truth is that he who is the only Son of God by nature, not by grace, took man to himself by grace into such a unity of person that he was also Son of Man.

Born of the Holy Spirit

37. For the same Jesus Christ, God's only-begotten, that is, only Son, our Lord, was born of the Holy Spirit and of the Virgin Mary. We know also that the Holy Spirit is a gift of God, a gift equal to the giver, and so the Holy Spirit is also God, no less than the Father and the Son. And by the fact that the human birth of Christ is from the Holy Spirit, what else is manifested but grace itself? For when the virgin asked the angel how what he had told her would come about, seeing that she knew no man, the angel replied *The Holy Spirit will come upon you, and the power of the Most High will overshadow you; therefore the child to be born will be holy; he will be called Son of God* (Lk 1:35). And when Joseph wanted to put her away on suspicion that she was an adulteress, knowing that it was not by him that she had become pregnant, the reply he received from the angel was *do not be afraid to take Mary as your wife, for the child conceived in her is from the*

Holy Spirit (Mt 1:20): that is, what you suspect is from another man is from the Holy Spirit.

The Holy Spirit is not father

12, 38. But are we to say that the Holy Spirit is the father of Christ the man in such a way that while God the Father begot the Word the Holy Spirit begot the man, and that the one Christ is from these two substances, Son of God the Father according to his nature as Word and Son of the Holy Spirit according to his humanity, since the Holy Spirit begot him of the virgin mother like a father? Who will dare to say this? There is no need to show by argument how many other absurdities would follow from this, since this is already so absurd that none of the faithful would be able to bear listening to it. So we acknowledge our Lord Jesus Christ, who is God from God but was born as man of the Holy Spirit and of the Virgin Mary, to be in both his substances,[43] the divine and the human, the only Son of God the Almighty Father, from whom the Holy Spirit proceeds.[44] How then can we say that Christ was born of the Holy Spirit if the Holy Spirit did not beget him? Is it because he made him, since insofar as our Lord Jesus Christ is God, *All things were made through him* (Jn 1:3); but insofar as he is human, he too was made, as the apostle says, *he was made from the seed of David according to the flesh* (Rom 1:3)?

But since that creature whom the Virgin conceived and bore, although he belongs only to the person of the Son, was made by the whole Trinity—since the operations of the Trinity are inseparable—why was only the Holy Spirit named in connection with his making? Must the whole Trinity be understood to operate whenever one of them is named in connection with a particular deed? It must, as can be demonstrated by examples. But we must not delay too long over this matter, for our question concerns how it is that we say born of the Holy Spirit[45] when he is in no way the son of the Holy Spirit. Similarly, the fact that God made this world does not justify us in calling it God's Son, or saying that it was born of God, but we can rightly speak of it as made or created or established or instituted by him, or other similar and suitable expressions. So in this case, while we acknowledge that he was born of the Holy Spirit and of the Virgin Mary, it is hard to explain how he is not the son of the Holy Spirit and is the son of the Virgin Mary; without doubt the Holy Spirit's relationship to him is not that of a father, while the Virgin's relationship to him is that of a mother.

The meaning of sonship

39. So it should not be conceded that anything that is born of another thing is inevitably to be called its son. I do not wish to mention the fact that a hair, a louse, and a tapeworm are born from a person in a different way from a son, and that none of these is a son. I do not wish to mention them, because it is not suitable to compare them to something so great, but certainly nobody can rightly speak of those who are born of water and the spirit as sons of water,[46] but they are clearly called sons of God the Father and of Mother Church. So it was in a similar way that he was born of the Holy Spirit, the Son of God the Father, not of the Holy Spirit. For what we said about hair and other things is valuable only to show that not everything that is born of someone can also be called that person's son, just as not everybody who is called a person's son was necessarily born from that person, as is the case with those who are adopted.

And people are called "sons of hell,"[47] not because they were born from there but because they are being prepared to go there, just as the sons of the kingdom are being prepared for the kingdom.[48]

The Gift of God

40. So just as a thing can be born from somebody without being that person's son, and not everybody who is called a son is born of the person whose son he is called, clearly the manner in which Christ was born of the Holy Spirit not as a son and of the Virgin Mary as a son shows us the grace of God by which a man, without any preceding merits, at the very beginning of his natural existence, was joined to the Word of God in so great a personal unity that the Son of God was Son of Man and the Son of Man Son of God, and thus in the assumption of human nature grace itself, which cannot allow any sin, became in some way natural to that man. It was right that this grace should be signified by mention of the Holy Spirit because his mode of being God is such that he is also called the Gift of God: to say enough about that, if it were possible, would demand a truly lengthy discussion.[49]

Jesus was called sin

13, 41. His begetting or conception, then, was not due to the pleasure of carnal concupiscence,[50] and so he contracted no sin from his origin, and by God's grace he was joined and united in a wonderful and indescribable way in unity of person to the unbegotten word of the Father, who is God's Son not by grace but by nature, with the result that he himself committed no sin, and yet because he came in the likeness of sinful flesh[51] he too was called sin,[52] and was destined to be sacrificed for the washing away of sins. In the old law, in fact, sacrifices for sins were called "sins."[53] He was the true sacrifice for sins, of which they were shadows. So the apostle after saying *we entreat you on behalf of Christ, be reconciled to God,* immediately added *For our sake he made him to be sin who knew no sin, so that in him we might become the righteousness of God* (2 Cor 5:20-21). He did not say, as some lying manuscripts would have it, "he who had known no sin made sin for us" as if Christ himself had sinned for us, but he said that the God to whom we were to be reconciled *For our sake he made him to be sin who knew no sin,* that is, to be a sacrifice for sins through which we might be reconciled. So he was sin that we might be righteousness, not our own righteousness but God's, and not in ourselves but in him, just as he revealed sin, not his own but ours, not in himself but in us, in the likeness of sinful flesh in which he was crucified, so that since there was no sin in him he might in some way die to sin when he died to the flesh in which was the likeness of sin, and although he had never lived the old life of sin, he might signify by his resurrection the restoration of our life to newness from the old death by which we were dead in sin.

The great mystery of baptism

42. This is the great mystery of baptism which is celebrated among us, that all who share in that grace may die to sin, just as he is said to have died to sin because he died to the flesh, that is, to the likeness of sin, and that they might have life by being reborn from the font, whatever their physical age, just as he had life when he rose from the grave.

43. For from a newborn baby to a decrepit old man, just as nobody is to be forbidden baptism, so there is nobody who does not die to sin in baptism. But babies die only to original sin, while older people die to all those sins that by evil living they have added to the sin they have brought with them from birth.

The use of the singular and plural

44. But they are also usually said to die to sin, although doubtless they die not to one sin but to all the many sins that they have committed on their own account up till then, whether by thought, word, or deed, since the plural is often signified by the singular, as when Vergil says,

And they fill the womb with an armed soldier,[54]

although they did this with a number of soldiers. And we read in our own scriptures *pray to the Lord to take away the serpent from us* (Nm 21:7): he does not say "serpents" although many serpents were plaguing the people to lead them to say this. And there are countless similar instances. But when the one original sin is signified by a plural, when we say that infants are baptized for the remission of *sins*, rather than the remission of *sin*, this is the opposite figure of speech, which uses a plural to signify a singular. For example, after the death of Herod come the words *for those who were seeking the child's life are dead* (Mt 2:20), not "is dead." And in Exodus it says *they have made for themselves gods of gold* (Ex 32:31), when they had made a single golden calf, about which they said *These are your gods, O Israel, who brought you up out of the land of Egypt* (Ex 32:4), again using the plural for the singular.

In Adam's sin there are many sins

45. However, even in the one sin which came into the world through one man and passed to all men, because of which even infants are baptized, we can understand there to be many sins, if the one sin is divided into its component parts. For there is pride there, by which the man preferred to be in his own power rather than God's, and sacrilege because he did not believe God, and murder because he cast himself down to death, and spiritual fornication, because the integrity of a human mind was corrupted by the persuasion of the serpent, and theft, because a forbidden food was wrongfully taken, and avarice, because he sought more than should have been sufficient for him, and all the other sins that can be discerned in this one crime by a person who considers carefully.

A person's rebirth

46. It is said, and not without probability, that infants are also liable for the sins of their parents, not only those of the first humans, but also those of the people from whom they were born. The divine judgment *I shall punish children for the iniquity of their parents* (Ex 20:5; Dt 5:9) certainly applies to them until they begin to belong to the new covenant by regeneration. This covenant was prophesied when it was said through Ezekiel that children would not receive the sins of their parents, nor would it be any longer said in Israel *The parents have eaten sour grapes, and the children's teeth are set on edge* (Ez 18:2). So the purpose of each person's rebirth is that whatever there is in him of sin that he was born with may be done away. For sins that are committed later through evil action can be healed also with penitence, as we

see happening even after baptism. This shows that regeneration was only introduced because of a fault in our generation which is such that even one conceived in legitimate matrimony says *I was born guilty, a sinner when my mother conceived me* (Ps 51:5). He did not here say "in iniquity" or "in sin," though he could rightly have said that, but he preferred to speak of iniquities and sins, because even in that one sin which passed to all men, and which is so great that by it human nature was changed and came under the necessity of death, there are found to be several sins, as I have shown; and there are the other sins of parents which, although they cannot make such a change to human nature, nonetheless bind the children with guilt unless the free grace and mercy of God comes to their help.

The sins of ancestors

47. But there would be good cause for discussing the sins of other parents, the ancestors of each of us from Adam down to our own fathers. We might ask whether each person who is born is implicated in the evil actions and the many faults found in his origins, so that the later one is born the worse is one's situation, and whether the reason why God threatens descendants to the third and fourth generation[55] about the sins of their parents is that in his mercy he tempers his anger regarding the sins of ancestors so that it extends no further than that, so that those on whom the grace of regeneration is not conferred are not too heavily burdened in their eternal damnation as they would be if they incurred guilt by reason of their origin for the sins of all their ancestors from the beginning of the human race and had to pay the just penalty for them. I am not so rash as to say whether or not any other statement about so great a

matter can be found in holy scripture after more careful search and discussion.

The one mediator between God and humanity

14, 48. That one great sin, which was committed in a place and state of life of such happiness with the result that the whole human race was condemned originally[56] and, so to say, at root in one man, is not undone and washed away except by the one mediator between God and humanity, the man Christ Jesus,[57] who alone was able to be born in such a way that he had no need to be reborn.

Jesus' example

49. Those who were baptized with the baptism of John, with which Jesus too was baptized, were not reborn, but by a kind of preparatory ministry of the one who said *Prepare the way of the Lord* (Mt 3:3),[58] they were made ready for him through whom alone they could be reborn. For his baptism is not in water alone, as John's was, but also in the Holy Spirit,[59] so that whoever believes in Christ is reborn in that Spirit by which Christ was born, and so needed no rebirth. That is why the Father's voice was heard over him when he had been baptized *Today I have begotten you* (Ps 2:7; Heb 1:5; 5:5),[60] speaking not of the one day in time when he was baptized, but of the day of changeless eternity, to show that that man belonged to the person of the only Son: a day that neither begins with the end of yesterday nor ends with the beginning of tomorrow is always "today." So he willed to be baptized in water by John, not that any sin might be washed away from him, but to show his great humility.[61] Baptism found nothing in him to wash away, just as death found

nothing in him to punish that the devil might be overcome and conquered not by power and violence but by truth and justice, and since he had most wickedly killed Christ who had committed no sin to deserve his death, he might fully deserve to lose those he justly held captive because of their sin. So he accepted both baptism and death out of firm purpose, not driven by pitiable necessity but moved by his merciful will that one man might take away the sin of the world just as one man brought sin into the world, that is, to the entire human race.

Rebirth in Christ

50. There is this difference: that one man brought one sin into the world, but the other one took away not only that one sin but all the other sins that he found had been added to it. That is why the apostle says: *And the free gift is not like the effect of the one man's sin. For the judgment following one trespass brought condemnation, but the free gift following many trespasses brings justification* (Rom 5:16). This is because that one sin which comes to men from their origin, even if it is their only sin, makes them subject to condemnation, while grace *following many trespasses* justifies a person who has committed many sins of his own in addition to that one which he has contracted from his origins in common with everybody else.

51. But what he says a little later, *just as one man's trespass led to condemnation for all, so one man's act of righteousness leads to justification and life for all* (Rom 5:18), shows plainly enough that there is nobody born from Adam who is not under condemnation, and that nobody is freed from that condemnation except by being reborn in Christ.

Baptized in Christ's death

52. When he considered he had said enough for that place in his letter concerning the punishment that came from one man and the grace that comes from one man, he went on to commend the great mystery of holy baptism in the cross of Christ that we might understand that baptism in Christ is nothing other than an image of the death of Christ, and that the death of Christ on the cross is nothing other than an image of the forgiveness of sins, so that just as he suffered a true death, in us there is a true forgiveness of sins, and just as his resurrection was true, so also is our justification true. For he says *What then are we to say? Should we continue in sin in order that grace may abound?* (Rom 6:1), having said earlier *for where sin increased, grace abounded all the more* (Rom 5:20). So he asked himself the question whether it is right to persist in sin in order to receive an abundance of grace. But he replied *By no means!* and continued *How can we who died to sin go on living in it?* (Rom 6:2). Then, to show that we are dead to sin, he said *Do you not know that all of us who have been baptized into Christ Jesus were baptized into his death?* (Rom 6:3). So if the fact that we have been baptized in the death of Christ shows that we are dead to sin, clearly infants who are baptized in Christ also die to sin, since they are baptized in his death, for no exception is made when he says *all of us who have been baptized into Christ Jesus were baptized into his death* (Rom 6:3). He spoke in this way to prove that we are dead to sin. But what is the sin to which infants die when they are reborn if not one they have contracted by being born? So what follows also applies to them: *Therefore we have been buried with him by baptism into death, so that, just as Christ was raised from the dead by the glory of the Father, so we too might walk in newness of life. For if we have been united with him in a death like his, we will certainly be united with him in a resurrec-*

*tion like his. We know that our old self was crucified with him so
that the body of sin might be destroyed, and we might no longer be
enslaved to sin. For whoever has died is justified from sin. But if we
have died with Christ, we believe that we will also live with him.
We know that Christ, being raised from the dead, will never die
again; death no longer has dominion over him. The death he died,
he died to sin, once for all; but the life he lives, he lives to God. So
you also must consider yourselves dead to sin and alive to God in
Christ Jesus* (Rom 6:4-11). At this point he had begun to
prove that we are not to continue in sin that grace may
abound, saying *How can we who died to sin go on living in it?*
(Rom 6:2) and, in order to show that we are dead to sin,
adding *Do you not know that all of us who have been baptized into
Christ Jesus were baptized into his death?* (Rom 6:3). So he
ended that whole passage just as he had begun it: he spoke
of the death of Christ in such a way as to indicate that
Christ too was dead to sin. To what sin? Surely to the flesh,
in which there was not sin but the likeness of sin,[62] which is
why the flesh is called "sin." So he says to those who have
been baptized in the death of Christ, in which not only
adults but also infants are baptized, he says *So you also* (that
is, like Christ) *must consider yourselves dead to sin and alive to
God in Christ Jesus* (Rom 6:11).

The mysteries of Christ

53. So whatever took place in Christ's crucifixion, his
burial, his resurrection on the third day, his ascension into
heaven and his sitting on the right hand of the Father was
done that the life that Christians live within these mysteries, which are historical facts and not merely mystical utterances, might be lived according to their pattern. It was
because of his cross that Paul said *And those who belong to*

Christ Jesus have crucified the flesh with its passions and desires (Gal 5:24); because of his burial *we have been buried with him by baptism into death*; because of his resurrection *so that, just as Christ was raised from the dead by the glory of the Father, so we too might walk in newness of life* (Rom 6:4), and because of his ascension into heaven and sitting at the right hand of the Father *So if you have been raised with Christ, seek the things that are above, where Christ is, seated at the right hand of God. Set your mind on things that are above, not on things that are on earth, for you have died, and your life is hidden with Christ in God* (Col 3:1-3).

To judge the living and the dead

54. But what we profess about Christ concerning the future, that he will come from heaven and judge the living and the dead, has nothing to do with our life as we lead it here, since it does not belong among the things that he has done, but among things to be done at the end of the world. It was concerning this that the apostle went on to say *When Christ who is your life is revealed, then you also will be revealed with him in glory* (Col 3:4).

55. But there are two ways in which we can understand his future judging of the living and the dead: by the living we can understand those whom his coming will find here not yet dead but still living in this flesh of ours, and by the dead those who have left the body or will do so before he comes; or else we can understand the living to signify the just and the dead the unjust, since the just will be judged as well. For sometimes the day of judgment is spoken of as something evil, for example *and those who have done evil, to the resurrection of condemnation* (Jn 5:29), and sometimes as something good, as when Scripture says *Save me, O God, by*

your name, and judge me by your might (Ps 54:1). It is by God's judgment that the good and the evil are separated, so that the good, who are to be delivered from evil, not lost with the evil, may be set at God's right hand. That is why he cries *Judge me, O God*, and then, as if to explain what he has said, *and defend my cause against an ungodly people* (Ps 43:1).

Faith in the Holy Spirit and the Church

The holy Church

15, 56. When we have said about Jesus the only Son of God, our Lord, what is appropriate in a brief confession of faith, we add, as you know, that we believe also in the Holy Spirit, to complete that Trinity which is God. Then we mention Holy Church, whence we may understand that the rational part of creation which belongs to the free city of Jerusalem[63] must be mentioned after the creator, that is, the supreme Trinity, for what has been said about Christ the man concerns the one person of God's only Son. Therefore due order in the profession of faith required that the Church should be named after the Trinity, like a house after the one who lives in it, a temple after its god and a city after its founder. Here the whole Church should be understood to be meant, not only the part that is on pilgrimage on earth, praising the name of the Lord from the rising of the sun to its setting and singing a new song after its old captivity, but also that part which has remained with God in heaven ever since its foundation and has never suffered any fall into evil. This part is found among the holy angels and continues in blessedness, giving generous help as it should to its comrades who are on pilgrimage, since they will together form one company in eternity, which is one already by the bond of charity, established to worship the one God.

So neither the whole Church nor any part of it desires to be worshipped instead of God, nor does anybody want to be a god to those who belong to the temple of God which is built of those made into gods by the uncreated God.[64] So the Holy Spirit, if he were a creature and not creator, would certainly be a rational creature—for rational creatures are the highest of creatures—and so would not be placed before the Church in the rule of faith,[65] since he also would be a member of the Church in that part of it which is in heaven, and would have no temple but be himself a temple. But he has a temple, of which the apostle says *do you not know that your body is a temple of the Holy Spirit within you, which you have from God?* (1 Cor 6:19). Of the body he says elsewhere *Do you not know that your bodies are members of Christ?* (1 Cor 6:15). How then can he not be a god, since he has a temple, or be less than Christ, since Christ's members are his temple? Nor is his temple different from the temple of God, since the same apostle says *Do you not know that you are God's temple?* and to prove this added *and that God's Spirit dwells in you?* (1 Cor 3:16). So God dwells in his temple, not only the Holy Spirit, but also the Father and the Son. The Son also said of his body, through which he became head of the Church that is among men, *so that he might come to have first place in everything* (Col 1:18), *Destroy this temple, and in three days I will raise it up* (Jn 2:19) For the temple of God, that is, of the whole supreme Trinity, is Holy Church, that is, the whole Church, in heaven and on earth.

The Church in heaven

57. But what can we say of the part of the Church that is in heaven? Only that nobody in it is evil, and that nobody has fallen from there or will fall in the future since *God did not spare the angels when they sinned, as the apostle Peter writes,*

but cast them into hell and committed them to chains of deepest darkness to be kept until the judgment (2 Pt 2:4).

Angels

58. But what that highest and most blessed society is like, and what are the differences in rank there according to which all are called angels as if by their common name, as we read in the Letter to the Hebrews *But to which of the angels has he ever said, "Sit at my right hand?"* (Heb 1:13)—which means that they are all called angels—and yet there are archangels there as well, let those who are able tell us, provided they can prove the truth of what they say. Let them say whether these archangels are also called powers, so that scripture says *Praise him, all his angels; praise him, all his powers!* (Ps 148:2) as if that were the same as saying "Praise him, all his angels; praise him, all his archangels." And let them explain the difference between the four words the apostle seems to use to refer to that entire heavenly society when he says *whether thrones or dominions or rulers or powers* (Col 1:16). I confess that I am ignorant of these things. Nor am I certain whether the sun and the moon and all the stars belong to that same society, although some people think that there exist shining bodies that do not lack sense or intelligence.

The bodies of angels

59. Furthermore, who can explain the nature of the bodies with which angels have appeared to humans, so that they can not only be seen but also touched, and they sometimes present visions not to people's physical eyes but to their spiritual eyes or to their minds, or say something not

outwardly to the ear but inwardly to a person's soul, being themselves also within the soul, as it is written in the book of the prophets *The angel who talked in me said to me* (Zec 1:9)—for he did not say "Who spoke to me" but *in me*; or they appear to people during sleep and speak with them as in dreams,—for we read in the gospel *behold an angel of the Lord appeared to him in a dream and said* (Mt 1:20)? These are the means by which angels indicate that they do not have bodies that can be felt: they raise the very difficult question of how the patriarchs washed their feet,[66] and how Jacob wrestled with an angel whose presence was so solidly tangible.[67] When such questions are asked, and each person tries to answer them as best he can, our minds are given useful exercise, if moderation is observed in the discussion and the error is avoided of those who think they know what they do not know. What need is there to affirm or deny these and similar opinions, or to define them with care, when no harm is done by being in ignorance of them?

Put our hope in God

16, 60. It is more necessary to judge and recognize when Satan *disguises himself as an angel of light* (2 Cor 11:14), lest he seduce us into some harm by his deceit. For when bodily sense deceives us, but without moving the mind from that true and right way of thinking which enables a person to live faithfully, there is no danger to our religious way of life; also, when he makes himself appear good and does or says things appropriate to good angels, even if he is believed to be good, this mistake brings no harm or danger to Christian faith. But when by these means he begins to gain control of what does not belong to him, then there is need for great vigilance in order to recognize him and refuse to follow him.

But how many people are able to escape all his deadly tricks without the guidance and protection of God? This very difficulty is useful in ensuring that a person does not put hope in himself or in somebody else but rather in God, the hope of all who belong to him: surely none of the faithful doubts that this profits us more.

The pilgrim Church

61. So this Church which exists among the holy angels and powers of God will be known to us as it is when we are joined with it at the end to share in unending blessedness. But this Church, which is wandering on earth in separation from the other, is better known to us because we are within it, and because it is composed of human beings like ourselves. It has been redeemed from all sin by the blood of the mediator who has no sin, and of him it is said *If God is for us, who is against us? He who did not withhold his own Son, but gave him up for all of us* (Rom 8:31-32). Christ did not die for the angels, but the redemption and liberation from evil of any human by his death benefits the angels since such a person in a sense returns into good relations with them after the enmity caused between men and the holy angels by sins, and by the redemption of men the losses caused by the fall of the angels are made good.

Reconciliation on earth and in heaven

62. The holy angels, taught by God the eternal contemplation of whose truth is the source of their blessedness, know how large a number of members of the human race is required to complete that city. That is why the apostle says *to renew all things in Christ, things in heaven and things on earth*

(Eph 1:10). The things in heaven are made new when the loss caused by the fall of angels from heaven is made good from among men; and things on earth are restored when men themselves, predestined to eternal life, are freed from their old corruption and made new. And thus through the unique sacrifice in which the mediator was immolated, which the many sacrifices of the old law prefigured, things in heaven are reconciled with things on earth, and things on earth with things in heaven. For, as the same apostle says, *For in him all the fullness of God was pleased to dwell, and through him God was pleased to reconcile to himself all things, whether on earth or in heaven, by making peace through the blood of his cross* (Col 1:19-20).

Peace through the blood of the cross

63. This peace, as it is written,[68] surpasses all understanding, and we can only know it by coming to it. How do things in heaven receive peace, if not with us, that is, by being reconciled with us? Peace is always there, both among all the intelligent creatures and between them and their Creator. This peace surpasses all understanding, as has been said, but that means our understanding, not that of those who always see the face of the Father. But we, however great our human understanding, know in part, and see *in a mirror, dimly* (1 Cor 13:9.12). But when we are equal with the angels of God,[69] then we shall see face to face as they do, and we shall be as much at peace with them as they are with us, for we shall love them as much as we are loved by them. So we shall know their peace, since our own peace will be like theirs and as great, nor will it then surpass our understanding. But the peace of God, which is offered to us in that place, will without doubt surpass both our understanding

and theirs. From him every rational creature that is blessed receives its blessedness, but he does not receive his blessedness from them. So it is better to understand the words of scripture *the peace of God, which surpasses all understanding* (Phil 4:7) not excluding from that "all" even the understanding of the holy angels, but only that of God, for not even his peace surpasses his understanding.

Faith in the Forgiveness of Sins

The forgiveness of sins

17, 64. Even now, however, the angels are in concord with us when our sins are forgiven. So in our confession of faith the forgiveness of sins comes next in order after mention of the holy Church. It is because of this that the Church on earth stands, because of this that what was lost is found and does not perish.[70] With the exception of the gift of baptism, which has been given to us against original sin, so that what was contracted through birth might be taken away through rebirth—and it also takes away actual sins which it finds to have been committed whether in the heart or the mouth or in deed—with the exception of this great forgiveness, the beginning of man's regeneration in which all guilt whether inborn or acquired is removed, the rest of our life once we have come to the age when we can use our reason, however rich it may be in fruits of justice, is not lived without forgiveness of sins, since God's children, for as long as they live this mortal life, are in conflict with death. And although it is truly said of them *For all who are led by the Spirit of God are children of God* (Rom 8:14), they are moved by God's Spirit and they journey toward God as children of God in such a way that like children of men they fall back on themselves under certain human impulses even in their spirit, especially since it is weighed down by the corruptible body, and so they sin. But there are differences of degree, since although every crime is a sin, not every sin is a crime. Hence we say that the lives of holy men, for as long as they live in this death,[71] can be found to be without crime, but the great apostle says *If we say that we have no sin, we deceive ourselves, and the truth is not in us* (1 Jn 1:8).

Special times of penance

65. But we should not despair of God's mercy for the forgiveness of actual crimes, however great, in the holy Church for those who do penance, each in a way appropriate to his sin. But in works of penance, when a sin has been committed of such a kind that he who committed it is also cut off from the body of Christ,[72] time should not be measured so much as sorrow, since God does not despise a broken and contrite heart.[73] But because the sorrow of one heart is usually hidden from another, and does not become known to others either by words or by any other signs, although it is known to him to whom it is said *my sighing is not hidden from you* (Ps 38:9), times of penance are rightly established by those who govern the Church, that satisfaction may be made also to the Church, in which sins themselves are forgiven. Indeed, outside the Church they are not forgiven, for it is the Church that has received the Holy Spirit as her own as a pledge[74] without which no sins are forgiven in such a way that those to whom they are forgiven receive eternal life.

The future judgment

66. The forgiveness of sins in this life is chiefly because of the future judgment. The words of scripture *a heavy yoke is upon the sons of Adam from the day they come forth from their mother's womb till the day they are buried in the mother of all* (Sir

40:1) are so true that we see even infants tormented by various evils after the washing of rebirth: from this we should understand that everything that is done in the sacraments of salvation is concerned more with the hope of good things to come than with retaining or gaining good things in the present. Many sins are pardoned here and not avenged with any punishment, but their penalties are reserved for the future—and it is not in vain that the day when the judge of the living and the dead will come has as its proper name the Day of Judgment—just as on the contrary there are some sins that are punished here, and if they are forgiven they will certainly do no harm in the world to come. That is why the apostle says concerning certain temporal punishments imposed on those who sin in this life, to those whose sins are forgiven and not reserved for the final judgment, *But if we judged ourselves, we would not be judged by the Lord. But when we are judged by the Lord, we are disciplined so that we may not be condemned along with this world* (1 Cor 11:31-32).

Faith and good works

18, 67. There are some who believe that also those who are baptized with Christ's cleansing and do not desert his name nor are cut off from him by any heresy or schism, however great the sins in which they live without washing them away with penitence or redeeming them with acts of charity, but persisting in them most tenaciously until the last day of this life, will be saved by fire, although because of the greatness of their sins and wickednesses this will be after they have been punished with a fire that lasts for a long time, but not for eternity. But it seems to me that people who believe this, Catholic though they are, are deceived by a certain humane good will. When we consult holy scripture, it gives us a different reply. I have written a book about this question, with the title *Faith and Works*,[75] where I have demonstrated as best I might with God's help how according to the holy scriptures the faith that saves is the one the apostle Paul described plainly enough when he said *For in Christ Jesus neither circumcision nor uncircumcision counts for anything; the only thing that counts is faith working through love* (Gal 5:6). But if faith works evil rather than good, without doubt, as the apostle James says, it *is dead in itself* (Jas 2:17), and he also says, *if a person says he has faith, but does not have works, will faith be able to save him?* (Jas 2:14).

Furthermore, if a wicked man will be saved purely by fire, and this is how we are to understand the words of blessed Paul *he will be saved, but only as through fire* (1 Cor 3:15), then faith will be able to save without works, and the words of his fellow-apostle James will be untrue. Also Paul's own words will be false when he says *Do you not know that wrongdoers will not inherit the kingdom of God? Do not be deceived! Fornicators, idolaters, adulterers, male prostitutes, sodomites, thieves, the greedy, drunkards, revilers, robbers—none of these will inherit the kingdom of God* (1 Cor 6:9-10). If those who persist in these sins will nonetheless be saved because of faith in Christ, how is it that they will not be in the kingdom of God?

Saved by fire

68. But since these utterances of the apostles, most plain and clear as they are, cannot be false, the obscure saying about those who build on the foundation that is Christ not with gold, silver, or precious stones, but with wood, clay, and straw[76]—for it is of these that it is said that they will be saved by fire, since by virtue of their foundation they will

not perish—must be understood in a way that does not contradict those plain statements.

By wood, clay, and straw we can reasonably understand desires for worldly things, although they are granted to us as lawful, so strong that they cannot be lost without mental agony. And since such agony burns us, if Christ's foundation is in our heart, that is, in such a way that nothing is put before him, and a person on fire with this agony would rather be deprived of the things he so loves than be deprived of Christ, he is saved by fire. But if in the time of temptation he prefers to hold on to such temporal, worldly things rather than to Christ, he has not Christ in his foundation, since he gives these the first place, and nothing in a building comes before the foundation.

The fire of which the apostle speaks in that place must be understood to be of such a kind that both pass through it, those who build on this foundation with gold, silver and precious stones, and those who build with wood, clay, and straw, for after those words he added *the fire will test what sort of work each has done. If what has been built on the foundation survives, the builder will receive a reward. If the work is burned up, the builder will suffer loss; the builder will be saved, but only as through fire* (1 Cor 3:13-15). So fire will test the work, not only of one of the groups, but of both. The test of tribulation is one kind of fire, of which scripture speaks openly in another place: *The kiln tests the potter's vessels, and the trial of tribulation the just man* (Sir 27:6).[77]

This fire has in this intermediate life the effect the apostle spoke of if it comes to two of the faithful, one thinking of the things of God and how he may please God,[78] that is, building on the foundation that is Christ with gold, silver, and precious stones, while the other thinks of the things of the world, how he may please his wife,[79] that is, building on the same foundation with wood, clay, and straw. For the

work of the former is not burnt up, since he did not love
things whose loss causes him pain. But the work of the latter is burnt up, since the loss of things we possess with love
never happens without pain; but since, given the choice, he
would rather lose them than Christ, nor does he desert
Christ out of fear of losing them, although he is grieved by
their loss, he is saved, but as if by fire, for the pain of losing
things he loves burns him, but without ruining or consuming him, since he has the protection of a foundation that is
firm and without decay.

Purifying fire

69. Nor is it beyond belief that something of the same
kind could happen also after this life, and it can be asked if
it is the case, whether or not an answer can be found, that
some of the faithful are saved by a purifying fire,[80] more or
less quickly depending on whether they have loved perishable good things more or less; but this does not apply to
those of whom it is said that they will not possess the kingdom of God,[81] unless those sins are forgiven them and they
do suitable penance. By "suitable" I mean that they should
not be sterile in works of charity, to which holy scripture at-
taches so much importance that the Lord says he will consider only the fruitfulness in such works of those on his
right and the sterility in them of those on his left when he
says to the former *Come, you that are blessed by my Father, inherit the kingdom* (Mt 25:34), and to the latter *depart into the
eternal fire* (Mt 25:41).

Works of charity

19, 70. Certainly nobody should think that those unmentionable crimes whose perpetrators will not possess the kingdom of God should be committed every day and expiated every day by works of charity. We should amend our lives, and do good works to beg God's mercy for our past sins, not try to buy him in some way so as always to be able to do such things with impunity. He has never given anybody freedom to sin, although in his mercy he cancels the sins we have already committed, provided we do not neglect to make appropriate satisfaction.

The Lord's Prayer

71. As for the daily brief and unimportant sins without which it is impossible to lead this life, the daily prayer of the faithful makes satisfaction for them. Their prayer is *Our Father in heaven*, since they have already been reborn as children of a heavenly Father by water and the Holy Spirit.[82] This prayer entirely cancels tiny daily sins. It also cancels those from which the faithful turn away by penance and reform, even though they have lived wickedly, provided that, as they truthfully pray *forgive us our sins*—for they have no lack of sins to be forgiven—they are also speaking the truth when they say *as we forgive those who sin against us*, that is, provided what they say is what they do, for to forgive a person who asks for pardon is itself a work of charity.

Giving alms

72. And so the Lord's words *Give alms, and everything is clean for you* (Lk 11:41) applies to any work of mercy that

benefits somebody. Not only somebody who offers food to the hungry, drink to the thirsty, clothing to the naked, hospitality to the traveler, asylum to the refugee, a visit to the sick or the prisoner, redemption to the captive, support to the weak, guidance to the blind, comfort to the sorrowful, medicine to the unwell, a path to the wanderer, advice to the uncertain, or whatever is necessary to a person in need, but also one who offers pardon to the sinner, is giving alms. And one who uses the whip to correct somebody over whom he has power, or disciplines him in some way, and yet puts away from his heart that person's sin by which he has been hurt or offended, or prays that it may be forgiven him, is giving alms not only through forgiveness and prayer, but also in reproof and correction by some punishment, for thus he is showing mercy. Many good things are offered to people unwilling to accept them when what is good for them is being considered rather than what they desire, because they prove to be their own enemies, while their true friends are rather those whom they consider enemies, mistakenly repaying them evil for good, whereas a Christian should not repay evil even for evil. So there are many kinds of alms, and when we do them we receive help for the forgiveness of our sins.

Love your enemies and will them good

73. But there is no almsdeed greater than forgiving from our heart a sin that somebody has committed against us. It is a lesser thing to be kind or even generous to a person who has done you no harm. Much greater, a sign of the most generous goodness, is to love your enemy also and to will good, and when possible to do good, to a person who wills you ill and does it if he can: when you do this you are listen-

ing to the voice of Jesus saying *Love your enemies, do good to those who hate you, and pray for those who persecute you* (Mt 5:44).[83] But this is a characteristic of perfect children of God, which every one of the faithful must strive for, training his human spirit in such love by prayer to God and discipline and struggle within himself, and since this great virtue is not possessed by as many people as those whose prayers we believe are heard when the prayer is made *forgive us our sins as we forgive those who sin against us* (Mt 6:12), without doubt the words of this promise are fulfilled when a person who has not yet progressed so far as to love his enemy nevertheless forgives from his heart one who has sinned against him and asks for forgiveness, since he himself also desires the forgiveness he asks for when he prays and says *as we forgive those who sin against us*, that is, forgive our debts when we ask as we forgive our debtors when they ask us.

Forgiveness from the heart

74. A person who pleads with one against whom he has sinned, if he is moved by his own sin to make his plea, should no longer be thought of as an enemy whom it is as difficult to forgive as it was when he was behaving as an enemy. But anybody who refuses to forgive from his heart one who asks forgiveness and repents of his sin should not think that the Lord forgives his sins, since Truth cannot lie. What hearer or reader of the gospel does not know who said *I am the truth*?[84] When he had taught us his prayer, he strongly emphasized the thought it contains by saying *For if you forgive others their trespasses, your heavenly Father will also forgive you; but if you do not forgive others, neither will your Father forgive your trespasses* (Mt 6:14-15). Anybody who does not wake

up on hearing such a clap of thunder is not asleep but dead; and yet he is able to raise even the dead to life.

Not just almsgiving

20, 75. Certainly those who live very wickedly, and take no care to correct their lives or morals, and yet never cease to give alms among their very sins and crimes, take comfort in vain from the Lord's words *give alms, and everything is clean for you* (Lk 11:41): they do not understand how widely these words apply. It is true that in the gospel is written *While he was speaking, a Pharisee invited him to dine with him; so he went in and took his place at the table. The Pharisee was amazed to see that he did not first wash before dinner. Then the Lord said to him, "Now you Pharisees clean the outside of the cup and of the dish, but inside you are full of greed and wickedness. You fools! Did not the one who made the outside make the inside also? But for the rest, give alms and see, everything is clean for you"* (Lk 11:37-41). Are we to understand this to mean that all things are clean to the Pharisees who have no faith in Christ, even though they have not believed in him or been reborn by water and the Holy Spirit, provided only they give alms in the way they think right? All are unclean who are not purified by faith in Christ of which it is written *in cleansing their hearts by faith* (Acts 15:9) and the apostle says *but to the corrupt and unbelieving nothing is pure. Their very minds and consciences are corrupted* (Ti 1:15). So how can all things be pure to the Pharisees if they give alms without faith? How can they have faith if they have refused to believe in Christ and be reborn in his grace? But still the words they heard are certainly true: *give alms, and everything is clean for you* (Lk 11:41).

Almsgiving is a work of mercy

76. A person who wishes to give alms as they should be given must begin from himself and give them first to himself. Almsgiving is a work of mercy, and the saying is very true *have mercy on your soul and please God* (Eccl 30:24). We are reborn in order to please God, who is rightly displeased with the sin we have contracted by our birth. These are the first alms we gave ourselves, for by the mercy of the merciful God we searched for ourselves in our misery, acknowledging as just his judgment which brought us to misery, of which the apostle says *the judgment following one trespass brought condemnation* (Rom 5:16), and giving thanks to his great love, of which the same preacher of grace himself says *But God proves his love for us in that while we still were sinners Christ died for us* (Rom 5:8): thus we also, judging rightly of our misery, and loving God with the love he has given us, lead holy and upright lives. The Pharisees, having neglected the justice and the love of God, used to tithe the tiniest items of their produce for the alms they gave,[85] and so they did not begin from themselves when giving alms or show mercy first on themselves. Because of this order of love it is said *You shall love your neighbor as yourself* (Lk 10:27). So after rebuking those who washed themselves outside but were full of greed and wickedness within, he taught them to purify themselves within by giving alms of the kind that a man should give himself first of all: he said *But for the rest, give alms and see, everything is clean for you* (Lk 11:37-41). Then, to show what he was urging them to do and what they did not care to do, that they might not think he knew nothing of their almsgiving, he said *woe to you Pharisees*, as if to say "I have exhorted you to give alms that will make everything clean for you, *but woe to you, for you tithe mint and rue and herbs of all kinds* (Lk 11:42); for I know about these alms of yours,

so do not think I was exhorting you about those, *and you ne-glect justice and the love of God*, the alms by which you could be cleansed from every inner defilement, so that the physical objects that you wash might also be clean to you." This is what "everything" means, both inner and outer things, as we read elsewhere, *first clean the inside, and the outside also will be clean* (Mt 23:26). But he did not wish to be thought to have rejected alms that come from the fruits of the earth, and so he said *it is these you ought to have practiced,* that is, justice and the love of God, *without neglecting the others* (Lk 11:42), that is, alms from the fruits of the earth.

God's mercy shall go before me

77. So let not people deceive themselves who think that by almsgiving, however generous, from their produce or any financial wealth they may own, they can purchase for themselves impunity to continue in great crimes and wicked sins. Not only do they commit such deeds, but they love them so much they wish to continue in them forever, provided they can do so with impunity. But a person who loves wickedness hates his own soul,[86] and one who hates his soul is not merciful to it, but cruel. By loving it by the world's standards he hates it according to God's standards. If he wished to give it alms that would make everything clean for it, he would hate it by the world's standards and love it by God's. Nobody gives alms of any kind without receiving what he gives from the one who lacks nothing. That is why it is said *His mercy shall go before me* (Ps 59:10).

Trivial and serious sins

21, 78. To distinguish between trivial and serious sins is a matter for divine, not human, judgment. We see that some have been pardoned and permitted even by the apostles, such as what the venerable Paul says to husbands and wives *Do not deprive one another except perhaps by agreement for a set time, to devote yourselves to prayer, and then come together again, so that Satan may not tempt you because of your lack of self-control* (1 Cor 7:5). It might have been thought that this is not a sin, that is, to have intercourse with one's spouse otherwise than for the purpose of having children, which is one of the goods of marriage, but even for physical pleasure, in order that incontinent people in their weakness may avoid the deadly evil of fornication or adultery or some other impurity which it is disgraceful even to speak of. So, as I have said, this might be thought not to be a sin, had he not added *This I say by way of concession, not of command* (1 Cor 7:6). But who could deny that this is a sin when it acknowledged by the authority of an apostle that a concession is made to those who do it? The case is similar when he says *When any of you has a grievance against another, do you dare to take it to court before the unrighteous, instead of taking it before the saints?* (1 Cor 6:1) and a little later *If you have ordinary cases, then, do you appoint as judges those who have no standing in the Church? I say this to your shame. Can it be that there is no one among you wise enough to decide between one believer and another, but a believer goes to court against a believer and before unbelievers at that?* (1 Cor 6:4-6).

Here it might be thought that to go to court against somebody else is not a sin, but only to wish the case to be judged outside the Church, had he not gone on to add *In fact, to have lawsuits at all with one another is already an offense for you* (1 Cor 6:7). And to prevent anybody excusing himself with the claim that his grievance is just, and that he is suffering a wrong which he wishes to have removed by judicial sentence, he at once meets such notions or excuses with the words *Why not rather be wronged? Why not rather be defrauded?* (1 Cor 6:7) to recall what the Lord says, *if anyone wants to sue you and take your coat, give your cloak as well* (Mt 5:40), and (in another place) *if anyone takes away your goods, do not ask for them again* (Lk 6:30). Thus he prohibited his followers from entering legal proceedings with others about worldly matters, and this teaching led the apostle to call that an offense. But from the fact that he permits such cases to be judged within the Church, but forbids them outside the Church in fearsome terms, it is plain that here too he is pardoning something allowed as a concession. Because of these and similar sins, and others that may be lesser, offenses in word and thought, the confession the apostle James makes by saying *For all of us commit many offenses* (Jas 3:2) shows that we must daily and often pray to the Lord and say *forgive us our sins*, and not be lying when we go on to say *as we forgive those who sin against us (Mt 6:12)*.

Some sins appear trivial but are serious

79. There are also some sins that might be thought very trivial were they not shown in the holy scriptures to be more serious than is thought. Who would think a person who said "you fool" would be *liable to the hell of fire* (Mt 5:22), had not Truth said so? But he at once applied medicine to this wound by adding a command that brothers should be reconciled, for the next thing he said was *So when you are offering your gift at the altar, if you remember that your brother or sister has something against you* (Mt 5:23) and so on.[87] Or who would realize how great a sin it is to observe days and months and

years and times, like those people who will or will not begin something on certain days or in certain months or years,[88] because they consider certain times favorable or unfavorable according to some empty human teaching, did not the fear of the apostle give us a standard to measure the seriousness of this evil when he says to such people *I am afraid that my work for you may have been wasted* (Gal 4:10-11)?

Habitual sins, great and terrible, seem trivial

80. We must also recognize that sins, however great and terrible, are thought to be small or non-existent when they become habitual, to such an extent that people think they should not only not be hidden but even proclaimed and advertised when, as it is written, *the wicked boast of the desires of their heart, and those who do evil are spoken well of* (Ps10:3). In holy scripture such wickedness is called a cry, as you read in Isaiah the prophet when he speaks of the evil vineyard *I expected him to do justice, but he did wickedness, I expected righteousness, but heard a cry!* (Is 5:7) and similarly in Genesis *How great is the cry of Sodom and Gomorrah!* (Gn 18:20), since not only did those sins already go unpunished among them, but also they were practiced publicly and almost officially. So in our days many evils, if not the same ones, have come to be openly and habitually practiced, so that we are afraid not only to excommunicate a lay person for them, but even to degrade a cleric. So when a few years ago I was expounding the letter to the Galatians, at the place where the apostle says *I am afraid that my work for you may have been wasted* (Gal 4:10-11),[89] I was compelled to cry out "Woe on the sins of men, which horrify us only when we are unused to them! But as for habitual sins, to wash away which the blood of the Son of God was shed, although they are so serious that

they cause God's kingdom to be entirely closed to those who commit them, we are often compelled to look on and tolerate them, and even to commit some of those we tolerate, and grant, O Lord, that we may not commit all of those that we are unable to forbid!" But I shall consider whether my immoderate sorrow caused me to speak somewhat incautiously.

Two causes of sins: ignorance and weakness

22, 81. What I shall now say is what I have also often said in several places in my shorter works: there are two reasons why we sin, either because we do not see what we ought to do, or because we do not do what we know ought to be done: the first of these evils comes from ignorance, the second from weakness. We should fight against both of them. But we cannot win without divine help, not only to see what ought to be done, but in order that we may be healed and that pleasure in doing right may overcome within us the pleasure we take in things which we desire to have or fear to lose, which leads us to sin with knowledge and awareness. In this case we are not only sinners, which we were even when we sinned through ignorance, but also transgressors of the law, when we do not do what we already know should be done, or when we do what we already know should not be done. So we should pray to God not only that he will forgive us if we have sinned, which is why we say *forgive us our sins as we forgive those who sin against us* (Mt 6:12), but also that he will guide us so that we do not sin, which is why we say *And do not bring us to the time of trial* (Mt 6:13): for these things we should pray to him to whom it is said in the psalm *The Lord is my light and my health* (Ps 27:1), that his light may take away our ignorance, and his health our weakness.

For penance we need God's mercy

82. Penance itself, when there is a good reason for doing it according to the custom of the Church,[90] is often neglected because of weakness, for shame brings with it a fear of being ill thought of when we care more for the good opinion of others than for the righteousness that leads a person to humiliate himself in penance. So we need God's mercy not only when we do penance, but in order that we may do penance. Otherwise the apostle would not say of certain people *God may perhaps grant that they will repent* (2 Tm 2:25); and the evangelist tells us that, in order that Peter might weep bitterly, *the Lord turned and looked at him* (Lk 22:61).

Sin against the Holy Spirit

83. But anybody who does not believe that sins are forgiven in the Church, with contempt for this great and generous divine gift, and ends his last day obstinate in his opinion, is guilty of the unforgivable sin against the Holy Spirit, in whom Christ forgives sins. I have discussed this difficult question as clearly as I could in a small book I wrote solely for that purpose.

Faith in the Resurrection of the Body and Life Everlasting

The resurrection of the body

23, 84. As for the resurrection of the flesh, not that of some who have come back to life and then died again, but resurrection to eternal life like that of the flesh of Christ, I do not know how I can treat this briefly and answer all the questions that are usually raised concerning this matter. But a Christian must in no way doubt that the flesh of all human beings who have been born or are to be born, and have died or will die, will rise again.

85. The first question that arises in this regard concerns aborted fetuses, who have already been born in the wombs of their mothers, but not yet in such a way that they can be reborn. If we say that they will rise again, this may be a tolerable opinion concerning those that are already formed. But as regards unformed fetuses, who would not rather think that they perish entirely like seeds that have not been conceived?[91] But who would dare to deny, even though he may not dare to affirm it, that resurrection will supply anything the fetus lacks in form, and so that perfection that was destined to come with time will not be lacking, just as the defects that time would have brought will be absent, so that nature will not be deprived of anything fitting and suitable that time would have brought, or be defiled with things hostile and contrary to it that time has already brought, but

what was not yet complete will be completed, and what had been spoiled will be restored?

The beginning of life

86. And so a question that can be discussed in great detail among the most learned (and I do not know whether an answer to it can be found by human beings) is when a human being begins to live in the womb, and whether an infant has some kind of hidden life before it begins to move perceptibly. It seems to me to be too presumptuous to say that fetuses that are cut out and removed from the womb, lest by remaining there dead they might also kill their mothers, have never been alive. Now once a person begins to live, from that moment he is already able to die; and I cannot find a reason why a dead person, however death has happened to him, should be excluded from the resurrection of the dead.

Complete human bodies at the resurrection

87. For the same reason it will not be denied that seriously deformed babies that are born and live, however soon they die, will rise again, nor should it be believed that they will rise in the condition in which they were born, rather than with their nature healed and rectified. We should not think that the Siamese twins recently born in the East, whom many most trustworthy brethren claim to have seen, and about whom the presbyter Jerome of blessed memory has left us an account in writing,[92] will rise as one double person rather than as two people, which they would have been had they been born as true twins, just as all others born separately who are said to be physically deformed be-

cause they have an extra part to their bodies or one missing or some major deformity will be restored to a normal human form by the resurrection so that each soul will have its own body, and none will be joined together even though they may have been born joined together, but each will receive his own limbs separately so that all will have complete human bodies.

The material of the body never perishes

88. Nor does the earthly material from which mortal flesh is created perish in the sight of God, but whatever dust or ashes it may dissolve into, into whatever vapors or winds it may vanish, whatever other bodies or even elements it may be turned into, by whatever animals or even men it may have been eaten as food and so turned into flesh, in an instant of time it returns to the human soul that first gave it life so that it might become human, grow, and live.

89. So that earthly material that becomes a corpse on the departure of the soul will not be restored at the resurrection in such a way that those substances which seep away and are turned into one kind and shape of thing after another, although they return to the body they have left, will necessarily return to the same part of the body as they were in before. Otherwise if all the hair were to receive back what has been removed by frequent cutting, and the nails all that has been removed so often from them by paring, anybody who thought about it would form a picture of extreme and unsuitable ugliness, and be led to disbelief in the resurrection of the flesh. But as when a statue of somebody made of some destructible metal is melted by fire or ground into dust or molded into a lump, and a craftsman wants to restore it using the same quantity of material, it does not mat-

ter for the perfection of the statue which part of the
material is used for which part of the statue, so long as all
the material of which the statue was originally made is used
in the restoration, so God, the wonderful and indescribable
craftsman, will remake our flesh with wonderful and indescribable speed from all the material that had constituted it.
Nor will it matter for the flesh's restoration whether hair returns to hair and nails to nails, or whether some part of
them which had decayed is turned into flesh and other parts
of the body, for the providence of the craftsman will ensure
that nothing is done that is not suitable.

90. Nor does it follow that those who return to life will be
of different heights because they were of different heights
when they were alive, or that thin people will rise again as
thin as before and fat people as fat as before. But if it is in
the plan of the creator that each person retains his or her
distinctive and discernible appearance, while all are equal
in the other qualities of the body, the matter belonging to
each one will be modified so that none of it perishes and any
deficiency will be supplied by the one who was able to make
what he willed even out of nothing. But if there is a reason-
able inequality among the bodies of those who rise, like that
of voices in a choir, the bodily material of each person will
be transformed and fitted to the company of the angels,
with nothing that is unsuitable for them to perceive with
their senses.[93] Certainly, there will be nothing indecorous
there, but whatever will be will be suitable, and anything
unsuitable will find no place there.

91. So the bodies of the saints will rise again with no defect, no deformity, no corruption, burden, or difficulty, and
their facility in living will be equal to their felicity. That is
why they are called spiritual,[94] although there is no doubt
that they will be bodies, not spirits. But as we now speak of
an "ensouled" body, which however is a body and not a

soul, so then the body will be spiritual, while being a body and not a spirit. And as for the corruption which now weighs down the soul, and the vices which cause the flesh to have desires contrary to the spirit,[95] then it will be not flesh but a body, for there are also said to be heavenly bodies.[96] That is why it is said *flesh and blood cannot inherit the kingdom of God*, and the author goes on as if to explain what he has said *nor does the perishable inherit the imperishable* (1 Cor 15:50). What he previously called "flesh and blood" he subsequently called "corruption," and what he called "the kingdom of God" he calls "incorruption." But as for its substance, even then it will be flesh, which is why even after the resurrection the body of Christ is called flesh.[97] But that is why the apostle says *It is sown a physical body, it is raised a spiritual body* (1 Cor 15:44), because there will be such harmony between flesh and spirit, the spirit giving life without need of any sustenance to the body that will be subject to it, that nothing within us will fight against us, but just as we will have no external enemies, so we will not have to suffer ourselves as our own inner enemies.

The resurrection of the lost

92. As for those who are not set free by the one mediator between God and man from that mass of perdition which was caused by the first human, they also will rise again, each with his or her own flesh, but in order to be punished with the devil and his angels. Surely there is no need to expend effort in inquiring whether they will rise with the defects and deformities of their bodies and whatever defective and deformed limbs they had formerly. Nor should we weary ourselves by considering their appearance or beauty, since their damnation will be certain and unending. Nor is it of

interest to ask how their bodies will be incorruptible if they
are capable of suffering, or corruptible if they cannot die,
for there is no true life but a happy life, and no true
incorruption except where health has no pain to corrupt it.
But where an unhappy person is not allowed to die, so to
say, death itself does not die, and where perpetual pain
causes not death but torment, corruption is not at an end.
This is what sacred scripture calls the second death.[98]

Punishment in accord with guilt

93. But neither the first death, by which the soul is compelled to leave its body, nor the second, by which the soul is
not permitted to leave the body under punishment, would
have happened to human beings if nobody had sinned. Certainly the gentlest punishment of all will be for those who
have added no further sin to the original sin they have contracted; and as for those who have added further sins, the
smaller each person's wickedness here, the more bearable
will be his damnation there.

The will of the Almighty

24, 94. And so, while wicked angels and humans remain
in eternal punishment, the saints will know more fully the
good that grace has conferred on them. Then events themselves will demonstrate more clearly the truth of what is
written in the psalm *I will sing of mercy and of justice; to you, O
Lord, I will sing* (Ps 101:1) for nobody is set free except by an
undeserved mercy, and nobody is damned except by a judgment he deserves.

95. Then what is hidden now will no longer be hidden,
for of two infants one is to be taken up through mercy and

the other is to be left because of judgment,[99] and in him the one who is taken up sees what would be due to him by judgment if mercy had not come to his aid, and why he rather than the other was assumed, since they were both on trial in the same court, and why miracles were not performed in the presence of some people who would have done penance if they had been performed there, while they were performed in the presence of some who were not to believe. The Lord says quite plainly *Woe to you, Chorazin! Woe to you, Bethsaida! For if the deeds of power done in you had been done in Tyre and Sidon, they would have repented long ago in sackcloth and ashes* (Mt 11:21). Nor was God unjust in not willing to save them, since they could have been saved had they wished. Then will be seen in the clearest light of Wisdom what the faithful believe before it is seen openly, how sure, unchangeable and most efficacious the will of God is, and how many things he could do but does not will to do, while he wills nothing that he cannot do, and how true are the words that are sung in the psalm *Our God is in the heavens; he has done whatever he willed* (Ps 115:3). This is not true if there are things that he willed but did not do, or, what would be more unworthy, if what the Almighty willed was prevented from happening by the will of man. So nothing happens unless the Almighty wills it, either by allowing it to happen or by doing it himself.

The permission of evil

96. Nor should it be doubted that God does good even when he permits evil things to happen, for he does not permit this except by his just judgment, and clearly everything that is just is good. And so although evil things, insofar as they are evil, are not good, yet the fact that there are not

only good things but evil ones is good. For if the existence of evil things as well as good were not good, they would by no means be permitted to exist by the almighty good, for whom without doubt it is as easy to prevent things he does not will to exist as it is to do what he wills. If we do not believe this, the very beginning of our profession of faith is endangered, in which we confess our belief in one God the almighty Father. For the only true reasons why he is called almighty are that he can do whatever he wills, and that the effectiveness of the will of the almighty is not impeded by the will of any creature whatsoever.

The salvation of all

97. For this reason we must see how it is that we say what the apostle most truthfully said of God, *who desires everyone to be saved and to come to the knowledge of the truth* (1 Tm 2:4). Since not all are saved, but many more are not saved, it seems that what God wills to happen does not happen because a human will frustrates the will of God. When it is asked why not all are saved, the reply usually given is that it is because they themselves do not wish to be saved. This cannot be said of infants, who cannot yet either will or not will. If we thought we could attribute to their own will the babyish movements they make when they are baptized, we should say that they do not wish to be saved, since they resist as much as they can.

The words of the Lord in the gospel make the matter even clearer when he rebukes a wicked city with the words *How often have I desired to gather your children together as a hen gathers her brood under her wings, and you were not willing!* (Mt 23:37) as if God's will had been overcome by the will of men and the most mighty one was not able to do as he willed because the very weak prevented him by not being willing. Where is that omnipotence that has done whatever it willed in heaven and on earth[100] if he willed to gather together the children of Jerusalem and did not do so? Or was it rather the city that did not want her children to be gathered together by him? But he gathered together the children he willed to gather together despite her unwillingness, for in heaven and on earth he did not will some things and do them and will others but not do them, but he did everything he willed.

Grace alone distinguishes the redeemed from the lost

25, 98. Furthermore, who is so irreligious and foolish as to say that God cannot turn to good any of the evil wills of men he wishes, when and where he wishes? When he does this, he does it by mercy, and when he does not do it, it is by judgment that he does not do it, since *he has mercy on whomever he chooses, and he hardens the heart of whomever he chooses* (Rom 9:18). The apostle said this to commend God's grace, having already spoken about the twins in Rebecca's womb to whom, *before they had been born or had done anything good or bad (so that God's purpose of election might continue, not by works but by his call) she was told, "The elder shall serve the younger"* (Rom 9:11-13).[101] For this reason he quoted the other prophecy where *it is written, "I have loved Jacob, but I have hated Esau"* (Mal 1:2-3).[102] But realizing how this saying could strike those who cannot penetrate with their understanding the depths of this grace, he said *What then are we to say? Is there injustice on God's part? By no means!* (Rom 9:14). For it seems unfair that God should love one and hate the other without their deserving it by good or bad deeds. If in this discussion he had intended us to understand that God foreknew their future deeds, either Jacob's good ones or

Esau's evil ones, he would by no means have said *not by works* but "by future works" and would have resolved the question in this way, or rather, he would not have raised any question that needed resolution. But now, having replied *by no means!*, that is, by no means can there be unfairness with God, he immediately says, to prove that this happens without any unfairness on God's part, *For he says to Moses, "I will have mercy on whom I have mercy, and I will have compassion on whom I have compassion"* (Rom 9:15).[103]

Who but a fool could think that God is unfair, whether he passes adverse judgment on one who deserves it or shows mercy to one who is unworthy? Then he adds his own comment and says *So it comes not from the one who wills or runs, but from God who shows mercy.* So both those twins were born *by nature children of wrath* (Eph 2:3), not because of any deeds of their own, but being bound by the chains of damnation because of their origin in Adam. But he who said *I will have mercy on whom I have mercy* loved Jacob with gratuitous mercy, but hated Esau because of the judgment he deserved. And since this judgment by rights belonged to both of them, one brother learned from the example of the other that he should not boast of the difference of his merits, as if that saved him from receiving the same sentence in the same trial, but of the generosity of divine grace, since *it depends not on human will or exertion, but on God who shows mercy.* What I might call the entire face or countenance of the sacred scriptures is found by those who look well at it to warn us in its profound and saving mysteries that *the one who boasts should boast in the Lord* (1 Cor 1:31).

99. So, having commended the mercy of God by saying it depends not on human will or exertion, but on God who shows mercy, that he may commend his justice as well, since when mercy is not shown to a person this is not unfairness but judgment—as there is not unfairness with

God—he at once went on to add *For the scripture says to Pha-raoh, "I have raised you up for the very purpose of showing my power in you, so that my name may be proclaimed in all the earth"* (Rom 9:17).[104] Having said this, he ends by speaking of both, that is, mercy and judgment, saying *So then he has mercy on whomever he chooses, and he hardens the heart of whom-ever he chooses* (Rom 9:18). That is, he has mercy in his great generosity, and he hardens the heart without any unfair-ness, so that one who has been set free should not boast of his merits, nor should one who has been damned complain, except of his lack of merits. For grace alone distinguishes the redeemed from the lost, who have been formed into one mass of perdition by a cause common to all which they draw from their origin. But if anybody understands this in such a way as to say *"Why then does he still find fault? For who can re-sist his will?"* (Rom 9:19), as if it did not seem that an evil person should be blamed, since God *has mercy on whomever he chooses, and hardens the heart of whomever he chooses*, we should not be ashamed to give the reply that, as we see, was given by the apostle: *who . . . are you, a human being, to argue with God? Will what is molded say to the one who molds it, "Why have you made me like this?" Has the potter no right over the clay, to make out of the same lump one object for honor and another for dis-honor?* (Rom 9:20-21). There are some foolish people who think that here the apostle was lost for a reply and crushed the boldness of his opponent because he was at a loss for an explanation. But the words *who are you, a human being?* are very weighty, and in such discussions they recall human be-ings to consider their limitations with a brief phrase which in fact carries within it a very serious explanation, for a per-son who understands this can find no further reply to make. If he understands, he sees the entire human race con-demned in its traitorous root by God's judgment which is so just that even if nobody were to be released from that condemnation nobody would have any right to criticize God's justice. He sees also that it was necessary for those who are set free to be set free in such a way that from the large number who are not set free but are subjected to a condemnation that is entirely just it might be clear what the whole multitude deserved and where God's just judgment would lead even those who are freed if they had not the help of his undeserved mercy, so that *every mouth may be silenced* (Rom 3:19) of those who wish to boast of their own merits, and *the one who boasts may boast in the Lord* (1 Cor 1:31).

Good out of evil

26, 100. These are the great works of the Lord, *sought out according to all his purposes* (Ps 111:2, LXX), and sought out so wisely that when creatures, both angels and humans, had sinned, that is, had done not what he willed but what they willed, the creator fulfilled what he willed by means of that very will of the creature by which what was against his will was done, making good use even of evil creatures as befits the one who is supremely good, for the damnation of those whom he had justly condemned to punishment, and for the salvation of those whom he had mercifully predestined to grace. For as far as they were concerned, they did what God did not will, but as far as the omnipotence of God is concerned, they were in no way able to contravene his will. By the very fact that they acted against his will, his will was done through them. For the great works of the Lord are sought out according to all his purposes in order that even what happens against his will should in a wonderful and inexplicable way not be done despite his will, since it would not happen if he did not permit it, and he does not permit things unwillingly but willingly; nor would he in his goodness allow anything evil to happen were he not able in his omnipotence even to bring good out of evil.

101. But sometimes a human being wishes with a good will something that God does not will, even though God's will is more fully and certainly good—since his will can never be evil—as when a good son wants his father to live, while God in his good will wills that he should die. Again, it can happen that a human wills with an evil will what God wills with his good will, as when a bad son wishes his father to die, and God wills that also. Certainly the former person wills what God does not will while the latter wills what God does will, and yet the devotion of the former is more in harmony with the good will of God, although he wills something different from God, than the disloyalty of the latter, who wills the same as God.

In order to judge whether a person's will is good or bad, we need only know what it befits man to will and what it befits God to will, and to what end each person directs his will. For God fulfills some of his purposes, which of course are good, through the evil wills of evil humans, as when by means of ill-willed Jews, in accordance with the good will of the Father, Christ was killed for us, a good so great that when the apostle Peter did not wish it to happen, he was called Satan by the very one who was on his way to be killed.[105] How good to all appearances were the wills of the faithful believers who did not wish the apostle Paul to go to Jerusalem[106] so that he might avoid the sufferings that the prophet Agabus had predicted! And yet God wanted him to undergo those things to proclaim the Christian faith, making him a witness to Christ. And God did fulfill that good will of his through the good wills of Christians but also through the evil wills of Jews, and those who did not will what God willed belonged to God more than those through whose evil wills what he willed was done, for they did the same deed, but they did it with an evil will while God did it through them with a good will.

102. But however many wills there are whether of angels or humans, good or evil, willing the same as God or differently, the will of the Almighty is always undefeated: it can never be evil, for even when it commands evils it is just, and clearly what is just is not evil. So almighty God either in his mercy shows mercy to whom he will or through justice hardens whom he will, and never does anything unfairly or unwillingly, and does everything that he wills.[107]

The meaning of 1 Timothy 2:4

27, 103. And so when we hear and read in the sacred scriptures that God wills everyone to be saved, although we are certain that not everybody is saved, we should not for that reason envisage any limitation to the will of almighty God, but understand the words of scripture *who wills everyone to be saved* (1 Tm 2:4) as meaning that nobody is saved except those whom he wills to be saved, not because there is nobody whom he does not will to be saved, but because nobody is saved except those whom he wills to be saved, and so we should pray him to will, for what he wills must necessarily come about. The apostle was speaking about praying to God, and that led him to say those words. We must also understand in a similar way the words of the gospel *who enlightens everyone who comes* (Jn 1:9), not that there is nobody who is not enlightened, but that nobody is enlightened except by him. Or in any case who wills everyone to be saved is said not because there is nobody whom he does not will to be saved, he who did not will to perform deeds of power in the presence of people who he said would have done penance if he had performed them,[108] but in order that we might understand by everyone the whole race of human-kind in all its diversity, kings and private citizens, nobles and commoners, important people and humble ones, the learned and the uneducated, the healthy and the weak, the clever, the slow-witted, the foolish, the rich, the poor and those of moderate means, men and women, infants, children, adolescents, young people, middle-aged people, old people, of all languages and customs, skills and professions, with their innumerable variety of desires and thoughts and everything else which makes human beings different from one another. Is there any group out of which God does not will that human beings of all races should be saved through his only Son our Lord, and so does not save them, for the Almighty cannot will in vain anything that he wills?

The apostle had urged that *prayers be made for everyone*, and had added in particular *for kings and all who are in high positions* (1 Tm 2:1-2), who might be thought to be repelled by the humility of the Christian faith because of the trappings of power and worldly pride. Then, saying *This is right and is acceptable in the sight of God* (1 Tm 2:3), that is, to pray for such people, he immediately added as a remedy against despair *who wills everyone to be saved and to come to the knowledge of the truth* (1 Tm 2:4). God has judged it good that he should deign to give salvation to important people through the prayers of the humble, which we see has already been fulfilled. The Lord used the same way of speaking in the gospel when he said to the Pharisees *you tithe mint and rue and all herbs* (Lk 11:42), since not even the Pharisees tithed all the herbs belonging to others and all the herbs of all the other nations throughout the earth. So just as here all herbs means every kind of herb, so there we can understand *everyone* to mean every race of humanity. And it can be understood in any other way, provided we are not compelled to believe that the Almighty willed anything to happen that did not happen; if, as the Truth sings without any ambiguity, *he has done whatever he willed* (Ps 115:3) in heaven and on earth, then plainly whatever he has not done he has not willed to do.

The first human being

28, 104. So God would have willed to preserve even the first man in that healthy state in which he had been created, and at the appropriate time after he had had children to bring him to better things without the intervention of death, where he would be unable not only to sin but even to will to sin, had God foreknown that he would have a permanent will to remain without sin as he had been created. But because God foreknew that he would make evil use of his free will, God prepared his design[109] to bring good even out of one who did evil, so that man's evil will might not be made of no effect, but nevertheless the Almighty's good will might be fulfilled.

105. It was right that the first man should be made capable of willing both good and evil, not without reward if he willed good nor without punishment if he willed evil. But later his condition will be that he cannot will evil, nor will he for that reason be without free will. The will that is utterly incapable of serving sin will be much more free. For we should not blame the will, or say that it is not a will, or that it is not free, by which we so will to be blessed that not only do we not will to be wretched but we are entirely incapable of willing it. Just as our will even now is unable to will unhappiness, so it will forever refuse to will iniquity. But it was necessary to observe the order according to which God willed to show how good the rational creature is even when able not to sin, although it is better when it is not able to sin;

similarly, that immortality in which he was able not to die was real, although lesser than the future immortality in which he will be unable to die.

The mercy of God has been greater

106. The former was the immortality that human nature lost through its free choice, while the latter it will receive through grace and, had it not sinned, would have received through merit. However, even then that merit could not have existed without grace, for although sin depended entirely on the freedom of the will, free will was not strong enough to retain man's original justice without divine help and participation in the unchanging good. So just as it is within a person's power to die when he will—for there is nobody who cannot kill himself, for instance by not eating, to say no more—but the will is not enough for remaining alive without the help of nourishment and other things that support life, so man in paradise was able by his will to relinquish justice and so to destroy himself, but his will was not enough to retain the life of justice without the help of the one who had made him. But since that fall the mercy of God has been greater, since the will itself has also to be released from slavery, ruled over as it is by sin and death. Its liberation comes not at all from itself but only through the grace of God which is in the faith of Christ: thus, as it is written, *the will* itself *is prepared by the Lord* (Prv 8:35, LXX), and by the will man gains the other gifts of God through which he comes to an eternal reward.

Eternal life is the reward for good works

107. So the apostle gives the name of a free gift of God to eternal life itself, which is certainly a reward for good works, when he says *For the wages of sin is death, but the free gift of God is eternal life in Christ Jesus our Lord* (Rom 6:23). Wages are due payment for military service, not a gift, and so he said *the wages of sin is death*, to show that death rightly followed sin, not undeservedly. But grace is not grace unless it is free.[110] So it should be understood that even a person's meritorious good deeds are gifts of God, and when eternal life is given in payment for them, what is that but grace given in return for grace? So man was made upright[111] so that he might remain in that uprightness not without divine help, or be perverted through his own will. Whichever of these he chose, God's will would be done, either by him or certainly concerning him. So because he preferred to do his own will rather than God's, God's will concerning him was done, and God makes out of the mass of perdition that has flowed from his stock some vessels of honor and some of dishonor;[112] the vessels of honor he makes through his mercy, those of dishonor through his justice, so that nobody may boast of humanity, and consequently nobody may boast of himself.

A God had to be mediator

108. For we would not be freed even by the one mediator between God and man himself, the man Christ Jesus, if he were not also God. But when Adam was created, an upright man, there was no need of a mediator. But when sins had separated the human race far from God, it was necessary for us to be reconciled to God for the resurrection of our flesh

to eternal life by the mediator who alone was born, lived and was killed without sin, that human pride might be rebuked and healed by the humility of God and that man might be shown how far he had wandered from God when he was called back by God incarnate, and an example of obedience was offered to rebellious man by the man who is God, and when the only-begotten took the form of a slave which had previously deserved nothing the fountain of grace might be opened, the resurrection of the flesh promised to the redeemed might be foreshown in the redeemer himself, the devil might be vanquished by the very nature which he was rejoicing to have deceived, and yet man might not boast, lest pride might be born again, and anything else concerning the great mystery of the redeemer which can be seen or told by those who have made progress in the faith, or can only be seen, even if it cannot be told.

Between death and resurrection

29, 109. As for the time between a person's death and the final resurrection, souls are kept in hidden places of rest or of punishment depending on what each soul deserves because of the lot they won for themselves while they lived in the flesh.

110. Nor should it be denied that the souls of the dead are supported by the piety of their loved ones who are alive, when the sacrifice of the mediator is offered for them or alms are given in the Church. But such things only benefit those who during their lives have deserved that they would later benefit them. For there is a way of living that is neither so good that these things are not necessary after death, nor so bad that they are of no use after death: but there are those whose lives are so good that they do not need them,

and also those whose lives are so evil that after they have passed from this life even such things cannot help them. Therefore it is here that we accrue all the merit or demerit that can either support a person or weigh him down. But nobody should hope to gain in the sight of the Lord after death what he has neglected here. So the customs of the Church in praying for the dead are not contrary to the mind of the apostle who said *For all of us must appear before the judgment seat of Christ, so that each may receive recompense for what has been done in the body, whether good or evil* (2 Cor 5:10);[113] for even the possibility of benefiting from them was won by each person while living in the body. They are not beneficial to everybody. And why not, if not because of the differences between the life that each person lived in the body? So when sacrifices, whether that of the altar or sacrifices of alms, are offered for all the baptized who are dead, for the truly good they are acts of thanksgiving, for those who are not really good they are propitiatory, and for the truly evil, although they are of no help to the dead, they offer some kind of consolation to the living. And when they benefit somebody, they either bring full remission of punishment, or at least make the condemnation itself more tolerable.

The two cities

111. But after the resurrection, when the universal judgment is over and done with, the two cities will have their boundaries, one of Christ and the other of the devil, one of the good and the other of the wicked, both composed of angels and men. The former will have no will to sin and the latter no ability to do so, nor will either have any possibility of dying; the former will live truly and happily in eternal life, the latter will exist unhappily in eternal death without the

possibility of dying, for the condition of both will be without end. But among the former some will rank above others in blessedness while among the latter misery will be more tolerable for some than for others.

Future punishments cannot be denied

112. So it is in vain that some people, or rather most people, feel human sympathy concerning the eternal punishment and the unending, unremitting suffering of the damned, and so do not believe that it will happen. It is not that they argue against holy scripture but that of their own accord they soften what is hard and eliminate the harshness of an opinion concerning the damned which they imagine to be more terrible than true. God, they say, will not forget to be merciful or in his anger shut up his compassion.[114] We read this in a holy psalm, but without any doubt it should be understood with reference to those who are called vessels of mercy,[115] for they too are set free from their misery not because of their own merits but by God's mercy. But if they consider that these words apply to everybody, that does not mean that they must think the damnation of those of whom it is written *And these will go away into eternal punishment* (Mt 25:46) can be brought to an end, for otherwise the blessedness of those of whom the opposite is said, *but the righteous into eternal life*, would also be thought destined to end at some time. But let them think, if they so wish, that the pains of the damned are mitigated to an extent at certain intervals of time. This interpretation allows us to understand that the wrath of God, which is damnation—for that is what is meant by the wrath of God, not some disturbance in the divine spirit—remains on them[116] so that in his anger, that is, with his anger remaining, he still does not shut up

his compassion, not by bringing eternal punishment to an end, but by giving an alleviation or interruption of torment; for the psalm does not say "to end his anger" or "after his anger," but "in his anger." If that meant nothing more than the least it could possibly mean, to perish from God's kingdom, to be exiled from the city of God, to be cut off from the divine life, to be deprived of that abundant sweetness of God which he has laid up for those who fear him[117] and made perfect for those who hope in him, is such a great punishment that none of the torments that we know can be compared with it if it is eternal, however many centuries they may last.

Perpetual death of the damned

113. So that perpetual death of the damned which is separation from the life of God will last forever and will be the same for all, whatever views people may have because of their human feelings concerning varieties of punishment or alleviation or interruption of suffering, just as the eternal life of the saints will remain the same for all whatever the differences in honor of those who shine with one harmonious light.

Hope

Hope accompanied by holy charity

30, 114. From this confession of the faith, which is contained in short compass in the creed and is like milk for infants[118] when considered according to the flesh, but is food for the strong when spiritually meditated and reflected on, arises the good hope of the faithful which is accompanied by holy charity.[119] But of all those things that must be faithfully believed, the only ones that concern hope are those that are contained in the Lord's Prayer since, as the word of God attests, *Cursed are those who trust in mere mortals* (Jer 17:5), and consequently anybody who trusts in himself is bound by the chain of this curse. So it is only from the Lord God that we must ask for any good deeds we hope to do or any reward that we hope to receive for good deeds.

Seven petitions of the Lord's Prayer

115. It seems that in the gospel of Matthew the Lord's Prayer contains seven petitions, three of which are for eternal gifts and the remaining four for temporal ones, which however are necessary for acquiring the eternal gifts. What we ask for when we say *hallowed be your name, your kingdom come, your will be done, on earth as it is in heaven*—which some people have absurdly understood as meaning "in the body and in the spirit"—are certainly gifts that we must keep per-

manently: they begin here and as we progress they grow in us, but once they are perfect, which is something we must hope for in the next life, they will be possessed forever. But when we say *give us this day our daily bread, and forgive us our debts, as we also forgive our debtors, and do not bring us to the time of trial, but rescue us from the evil one* (Mt 6:11-13), who cannot see that these petitions concern our needs in the present life? So that eternal life in which we hope to be for ever, the hallowing of God's name, his kingdom and his will will endure perfectly and immortally in our spirit and body. But our daily bread is so called because we need it here in sufficient quantity to meet the needs of body and soul, whether we understand these words spiritually or carnally[120] or in both ways. Also it is here that the forgiveness of sins for which we ask belongs, for it is here that sins are committed: here are the temptations that lure or drive us to sin; here, finally, is the evil from which we desire to be delivered; but there none of those things exist.

Luke's five petitions

116. The evangelist Luke, however, included in the Lord's Prayer not seven but five petitions, not disagreeing with Matthew, but showing us by his brevity how Matthew's seven petitions are to be understood. The name of God is hallowed in the spirit, but God's kingdom will come in the resurrection of the flesh. So Luke, to show that the third petition was in a sense a repetition of the two preceding ones, made us understand it better by omitting it.[121] Then he added three others, for daily bread, the forgiveness of sins and avoidance of temptation. But he did not include Matthew's last petition, *but rescue us from the evil one*, in order to show us its connection with the preceding one which

concerns temptation. So he says *but deliver*, not "and deliver," as if to show it is one petition, "do not do this but that," so that each person may know that he is delivered from evil when he is not led into temptation.

Love

The primacy of love

31, 117. Now as for love, which the apostle says is greater than the other two, that is faith and hope,[122] the greater it is in a person, the better is that person in whom it is. For when we ask whether somebody is a good person, we are not asking what he believes or hopes for, but what he loves. For one who rightly loves without doubt rightly believes and hopes, and one who does not love believes in vain, even if the things he believes are true; he hopes in vain, even if the things for which he hopes are those which, according to our teaching, belong to true happiness, unless he also believes and hopes that if he asks he may also be given the ability to love. For although he cannot hope without love, it may be that he does not love that without which he cannot reach that for which he hopes, for instance if he hoped for eternal life—and who does not love that?—and did not love justice, without which nobody comes to eternal life. This is the faith of Christ, which the apostle commends to us, which works through love[123] and asks in love that it may be given what it does not yet have, seeks that it may find and knocks that the door may be opened to it.[124] For faith obtains by prayer what the law commands. Without the gift of God, that is, the Holy Spirit, by whom love is poured out in our hearts,[125] the law can command but not help, and moreover can make a transgressor of one who cannot offer ignorance as an excuse. Where the love of God is absent, there the cupidity of the flesh reigns.

The four stages of humanity

118. When people live according to the flesh, in the deepest darkness of ignorance, with no resistance from the reason, this is the first state of humanity. Then when knowledge of sin comes through the law, if the help of God's Spirit is not yet available, one who wishes to live according to the law is overcome and sins knowingly and becomes a slave of sin—*for people are slaves to whatever masters them* (2 Pt 2:19)—since knowledge of the law causes sin to *work every kind of concupiscence* (Rom 7:8) in humans, piling up transgressions so that what is written is fulfilled: *But law came in, with the result that the trespass multiplied* (Rom 5:20). This is humanity's second state. But if God turns again, so that we can believe that he helps us to obey his commandments, and a person begins to be *led by the Spirit of God* (Rom 8:14), he begins to desire against the flesh with the stronger love of charity, so that although the struggle continues of man against himself, since his sickness has not yet been entirely cured, nonetheless the one *who is righteous lives by faith* (Rom 1:17), and lives justly insofar as he does not give in to the evil of concupiscence because that is conquered by delight in justice. This is the third state of humanity, a good that is hoped for, and if a person perseveres religiously in this, peace awaits him at the end, which will be fulfilled after this life in repose of the spirit, and then also in the resurrection of the flesh. The first of these four states is before the law, the second under the law, the third under grace and the fourth in full and perfect peace. And this is how the life of God's people progressed through time, as it pleased God

who *disposes all things in measure and number and weight* (Wis 11:21). His people existed first before the law was given, then under the law that was given through Moses, then under the grace that was revealed by the first coming of the Mediator. However, grace was not lacking even earlier to those on whom it was right that it should be conferred, although it was veiled and hidden as God's dispositions for that period required. Except through the faith of Christ, not one of the just ones of old could find salvation, nor could he have been prophesied for us through their ministry, sometimes in a more open and sometimes in a more secret manner, had he not also been known to them.

The grace of regeneration

119. Whenever in any of what we may call those four ages the grace of regeneration has found out a single person, all his previous sins are remitted, and that guilt which he contracted by being born is removed by rebirth, although so true is the saying *the Spirit blows where it chooses* (Jn 3:8) that some have never known that second state of servitude under the law, but begin to receive God's help when they receive his commandment.

No harm to those who have received the sacrament of regeneration

120. Before a person can be capable of keeping the law, he must live according to the flesh. But if he has already received the sacrament of regeneration, he will receive no harm if he then passes away from this life, because Christ died and rose again that he might be Lord of the living and

the dead,[126] and the kingdom of death will not hold one for whom he, free among the dead, laid down his life.[127]

The end of the commandment is charity

32, 121. So all the divine commandments concern charity, of which the apostle says *the end of the commandment is charity that comes from a pure heart, a good conscience, and sincere faith* (1 Tm 1:5).Thus charity is the end of every commandment, that is, every commandment concerns charity. But what is done in fear of punishment or for any carnal reason, and not with reference to that charity which the Holy Spirit pours out in our hearts,[128] is not yet being done as it should be done, although it seems to be being done. This love is of God and our neighbor, and *On these two commandments hang all the law and the prophets* (Mt 22:40). Consider also the gospel and the apostles, for that is where we find the sayings *the end of the commandment is charity* and *God is love* (1 Jn 4:8). So whatever God commands, such as *You shall not commit adultery* (Ex 20:14; Dt 5:18), and whatever is not commanded but advised for spiritual reasons, for instance *It is well for a man not to touch a woman* (1 Cor 7:1), is rightly observed when it is done out of love of God and of one's neighbor because of God, both in this world and in the world to come, of God now through faith and then face-to-face, and of our neighbor now also through faith. For we mortals do not know the hearts of other mortals. But then the Lord *will bring to light the things now hidden in darkness and will disclose the purposes of the heart. Then each one will receive commendation from God* (1 Cor 4:5), because each will praise and love in his neighbor that which God has illuminated that it may not be hidden from him. As love grows, cupidity decreases until in this world that greatness is reached than which nothing can be greater, for *no one has greater love than this, to lay down one's life for one's friends* (Jn 15:13). But who can say how great love will be where there is no cupidity to restrain or overcome it? Nobody, surely, for where there is no battling with death, there health will be at its most perfect.

Epilogue

Conclusion

122. But there must come a time for this book to end, and it is for you to see whether or not you should call it a "handbook." But I, not thinking it right to spurn your eagerness for Christ, believing good of you and hoping for good from you with the help of our redeemer, and loving you greatly among his members, have done what I can to write this book *Faith, Hope, and Charity* for you, and I wish it were as useful as it is long.

Notes

Prologue

1. Some manuscripts add: Just as nobody can be the cause of his own existence, so nobody can cause his own wisdom, but wisdom comes from the enlightenment of the one of whom it is written *All wisdom is from God* (Sir 1:1).
2. See Gal 5:6.
3. See Acts 2:21; Rom 10:13.
4. Lucan, *Civil War* 2:15.
5. Vergil, *Aeneid* 4:419.
6. Note that Augustine does not attribute the Letter to the Hebrews to Saint Paul. By the time he wrote the *Enchiridion* he had come to regard it as anonymous. It was not universally regarded as part of the New Testament Canon in his day, whence his appeal in this sentence to other writers to justify his use of it as an authority.

Faith in God the Creator

7. The present Western version of the Nicene-Constantinopolitan Creed, widely familiar through its use at the Sunday eucharist, says that the Holy Spirit proceeds *from the Father and the Son*, although its original form, as approved by the Council of Constantinople in 381, spoke only of procession of the Spirit *from the Father*. The Western doctrine of the double procession of the Spirit was developed by Augustine and subsequent thinkers influenced by him. It is worth noting that here, although he speaks of the *Spirit of Father and Son*, he follows the pre-Augustinian pattern in speaking only of procession *from the Father*.
8. Vergil, *Aeneid* 10:100.
9. See Mt 12:35.
10. See Mt 7:16
11. *Georgics* 2:490: Vergil was speaking of the Greek philosopher Epicurus.
12. Vergil, *Georgics* 2:479.
13. In Latin, "to be mistaken" and "to lose one's way" are expressed by the same verb, *errare*.

137

14. A rigoristic sect named after their early leader Donatus, who denied the validity of sacraments conferred by those who had lapsed from the faith in times of persecution. Augustine spent much effort in controversy with them. They were associated with a rural terrorist movement, by one of whose cells Augustine was threatened in the episode he narrates here; see Possidius, *Life of Saint Augustine* 12.
15. Vergil, *Eclogues* 8:4.
16. That is, *Lying* (*De Mendacio*).
17. See Acts 12:9.
18. *Aeneid* 10:392.
19. A philosophical school named after the Academy, a building in Athens. They were noted for their skepticism.
20. See *Answer to the Skeptics* (*Contra Academicos*)
21. See Rom 1:17; Gal 3:11; Heb 10:38.
22. See Gal 5:6.
23. See Acts 12:9.
24. See Gn 37:33.
25. See Rom 8:17.

Faith in Christ the Redeemer

26. Augustine thinks of the whole human race as contained within Adam, since all come from his seed. Therefore, in hurting himself, Adam hurt his descendants.
27. This term is sometimes misunderstood. Original derives from the Latin *origo*, "origin": original sin belongs to us by reason of our origin.
28. Augustine's text was different from that of modern editions. This is how he would have translated it.
29. See Lk 20:36; *The City of God* XXII,1.
30. See Gal 4:26.
31. See Rom 4:17.
32. See 1 Cor 7:25.
33. See Eph 2:8-9.
34. See Eph 2:10.
35. See Prv 8:35, LXX.
36. See Mt 5:44.
37. See Mt 7:7.
38. According to the ancient doctrine of *virginitas in partu*, Mary remained physically intact throughout the process of childbirth.
39. See Letter 137.
40. See Jn 10:30.
41. See Jn 14:28.
42. See Phil 2:6-7.
43. Augustine uses the term "substance" where theology since the Council of Chalcedon has usually used the term "nature." However, "substance" was

regularly used in this sense by Latin theologians from Tertullian to Leo the Great.

44. Again, Augustine speaks of the Holy Spirit as proceeding only from the Father. See III, 9.
45. See Mt 1:20.
46. See Jn 3:5.
47. See Mt 23:15.
48. See Mt 8:12.
49. Augustine discusses this question at length in his book *The Trinity*.
50. Augustine seems here to leave open the possibility that the transmission of original sin is due to the pleasure of intercourse. He disowned this view in *Marriage and Desire*.
51. See Rom 8:3.
52. See 2 Cor 5:21.
53. See Lv 6:23; Nm 8:8; Hos 4:8.
54. Vergil, *Aeneid* 2:20. Vergil is speaking of the Greek soldiers inside the wooden horse by which they gained entrance to the city of Troy.
55. See Ex 20:5; Dt 5:9.
56. That is, at its origin: see VIII, 26.
57. See 1 Tm 2:5.
58. See Is 40:3; Lk 3:4.
59. See Mt 3:11; Mk 1:8.
60. See Mt 3:17. These words do not occur in any of the gospel narratives of Jesus' baptism.
61. See Mt 3:15.
62. See Rom 8:3.

Faith in the Holy Spirit and the Church

63. See Gal 4:26.
64. See Gn 3:5; Ps 81:6; Jn 10:34-35.
65. That is, the Creed, which was anciently known as the Canon or Rule of Faith.
66. See Gn 18:4; 19:2.
67. See Gn 32:24-25.
68. See Phil 4:7.
69. See Lk 20:36.

Faith in the Forgiveness of Sins

70. See Lk 15:32.
71. Augustine sees this life as a death in comparison with the life to come.
72. In the early Christian centuries, sinners would do public penance for a period before being readmitted to the communion of the Church.

73. See Ps 51:17.
74. See 2 Cor 1:22.
75. See especially *Faith and Works* 13.
76. See 1 Cor 3:12.
77. See Sir 2:5.
78. See 1 Cor 7:32.
79. See 1 Cor 7:33.
80. Latin *purgatorium*: Augustine's teaching in this section shows the doctrine of purgatory at an early stage in its development.
81. See 1 Cor 6:10.
82. See Jn 3:5.
83. See Rom 12:17-21.
84. See Jn 14:6.
85. See Lk 11:42.
86. See Ps 11:5, LXX.
87. Jesus' words continue *leave your gift there before the altar, and go first to be reconciled to your brother or sister, and then come and offer your gift* (Mt 5:24).
88. The Roman state recognized certain days as *dies nefasti*, on which business was forbidden for religious reasons.
89. See Augustine, *Exposition of the Letter to the Galatians* 35.
90. See XVII, 65.

Faith in the Resurrection of the Body and Life Everlasting

91. According to ancient biological theories, the female contributed nothing in conception except a receptacle for the growth of the seed contributed by the male.
92. Jerome, Letter 2 to Vitalis.
93. Augustine considered that angels had bodies, a view largely abandoned in later theology.
94. See 1 Cor 15:44.
95. See Wis 9:15; Gal 5:17.
96. See 1 Cor 15:40.
97. See Lk 24:39.
98. See Rv 2:11; 20:6.14.
99. See Rom 9:10-13.
100. See Ps 115:3.
101. See Gn 25:23.
102. See Rom 9:13.
103. See Ex 33:19.
104. See Ex 9:16.
105. See Mt 16:22-23.
106. See Acts 21:10-14.
107. See Ps 115:3.
108. See Mt 11:21.

109. See Prv 8:35, LXX: *The will is prepared by the Lord*.
110. See Rom 11:6.
111. See Eccl 7:29.
112. See Rom 9:21-23.
113. See Rom 14:10.
114. See Ps 77:9.
115. See Rom 9:23.
116. See Jn 3:36.
117. See Ps 31:19.

Hope

118. See 1 Cor 3:1-2.
119. See 1 Cor 13:13.
120. That is, with reference to the eucharist or to ordinary food.
121. See Lk 11:2-4.

Love

122. See 1 Cor 13:13.
123. See Gal 5:6.
124. See Mt 7:7.
125. See Rom 5:5.
126. See Rom 14:9.
127. See Ps 88:5.
128. See Rom 5:5.

Index